MY
WHAT
IF
YEAR

A MEMOIR

ALISHA FERNANDEZ
MIRANDA

Zibby Books
New York

My What If Year: A Memoir

Library of Congress Control Number: 2022939129
ISBN: 978-1-958506-09-7
eBook ISBN: 979-8-9862418-3-8

Book design by Ursula Damm
Cover design by Gabriele Wilson
Cover art © Shout
www.zibbybooks.com

Printed in the United States of America

To Carlos
You'll always be my number one

MY
WHAT
IF
YEAR

The story that follows is a memoir and is as accurate a recollection as can be expected by a tired, busy CEO, intern, and mother of twins in the middle of a global pandemic.

Any resemblance to persons or dogs living or dead is entirely intentional. Some names have been changed to protect the guilty, my frenemies, and terrible bosses.

Contents

Last night, while I lay thinking here,
Some Whatifs crawled inside my ear
And pranced and partied all night long
And sang their same old Whatif song

—"Whatif," Shel Silverstein

Chapter 1
From CEO to Intern

It all started innocently enough. I was mom-drunk, a unique form of inebriation exacerbated by the giddiness of being out for a night without your children. Like imbibing on medication or at high altitudes, it makes each cocktail feel like four.

Two of my best friends, Laura and Rebecca, were with me, also mom-drunk. Surrounded by contemporary art and sipping expensive rose-lychee martinis, we had come a long way from the warm kegs of our college nights together. The Coral Room at the Bloomsbury Hotel in London, where we were currently basing ourselves, was needlessly hip, a place where, you could tell, some of the best and worst decisions of people's lives were made. Tiered art deco chandeliers hung from the ceiling as people perched on plush pink banquettes at a gold-rimmed bar. The whole lounge smelled like jasmine and gin. We had a high table in the corner and our drinks and faces were reflected back at us in the mirrored glass surface.

My children were just across the river; Rebecca's kids were across the ocean. She had flown over from New York at the instigation of our friend Laura, who was on the English leg of her yearlong trip around the world. She and her husband had recently quit their high-profile jobs in Silicon Valley to travel with their six-month-old baby. They took pasta-making classes in Rome and pushed their stroller down the path by the Seine in Paris. They stayed in a Moroccan *riad* and made friends with a local rug seller from the market, who offered them a steep discount. Traveling with a baby had its challenges—the number of stomach bugs alone was enough to put you off—but for Laura, it was a life-changing experience.

"I'm just in awe," I told Laura, trying not to slur my words as I signaled to the bartender for another round of drinks. "I mean, you did it. You gave up everything and you're living the dream."

"Aren't you?" she countered.

Things did look that way. I was living in a house on a beautiful Georgian square in central London, a place that I had dreamed of living since the day I heard the first chords of "Wannabe" by the Spice Girls. I had an adoring husband, my sweetheart since we were twenty-two; a set of rambunctious and hilarious eight-year-old twins; and a French bulldog with a face made for Instagram. After years of working for other people, I had spent the last several as CEO of the social-impact company my husband and I cofounded. My job was rich with freedom and purpose. As the boss, I made my own schedule, often working from home and setting the corporate dress code as "business athleisure," and worked with incredible nonprofits, companies, and foundations around the world on how to do more good. I had everything I had ever wanted, or so I thought.

"I guess," I replied with a sigh.

"Well, what's your dream then?" Rebecca asked.

I didn't need to think about the answer—never had: "To be on Broadway, of course." They smiled knowingly. My love of musical theater was well known to both of them. We had spent four years in college showering in close proximity and they had heard me belt out "Don't Cry for Me Argentina" more times than I'm sure they'd care to remember.

"Okay, okay, for real, I think it's probably too late for my performing career," I said, feeling just the tiniest sting of disappointment at the truth of that statement. "But—I did have this weird idea. What if I could work backstage?"

I continued in detail. Even if I knew absolutely nothing about the process that goes into creating a production, I could, for example, fold thousands of preperformance *Playbills* or polish actors' tap shoes or even scrape gum off the bottom of the seats. I would do anything, really; I didn't care what. I just wanted to be a part of it.

Laura and Rebecca mulled it over as our martinis arrived at the table but both concurred: It would be awesome. "Like if you became an intern."

"Right," I said. "An intern. At practically forty."

It was weird how well these ladies knew me. Years ago, at seventeen, I had worked at *Ocean Drive* magazine in Miami Beach as an intern, harboring dreams of magazine journalism but really just filing celebrity photo slides (paparazzi shots) for two afternoons a week.

The internship had its perks. *Ocean Drive* was a Miami-based luxury lifestyle magazine that was approximately 95 percent ads and 5 percent hard-hitting, meaningful content like "Baring All: Bikinis, Maillots, and Monokinis, Oh My!" I was regularly invited to attend the parties that were too uncool for even the lowly junior editors—not movie premieres or after-parties fronted by world-famous DJs but events for things like the launch of a new Spanish-language search engine (Remember Yupi? Neither do I) or straight-to-cable movies starring Jean-Claude Van Damme.

In addition to going to C-list parties and getting the occasional free cosmo, I learned the ropes of magazine journalism. Filing hundreds of pictures of Britney Spears leaving The Coffee Bean & Tea Leaf and ordering them by date, I picked up some skills (for example, I can recognize any late 1990s/ early '00s celebrity in miniature—to this day I'm sure I would know Jessica Simpson if I saw her, very tiny, from a hundred feet away) and saw the inner workings of the entire enterprise.

More crucially, I had access—while making photocopies, retrieving coffees, and delivering smoothies for the editors. One day, after a particularly heated exchange with her boss, the assistant publisher turned to me as I dropped off her dressing-free salad and said, "Promise me you won't ever go into journalism. Everyone in this industry is a backstabber and will cut you down the moment they get the chance. Also, you'll never make any money."

Ocean Drive wasn't the professional mentorship I expected, but I took the unsolicited advice at face value. The magazine world wasn't for me but it was a broad and illuminating experience—one that taught me more in a short period of time than I think an entry-level job would have done.

That night at the Coral Room, plastered on vodka, I looked at Rebecca and asked (or possibly slurred), "What would *you* do? If you could do anything you ever dreamed for a few months?"

She considered, furrowing her eyebrows pensively. "Be a horse farmer," she said. "No, a producer on *Keeping Up with the Kardashians*."

Laura's ambitions were to try her hand at architecture or, conversely, at local government, which we noted was strange for a dream job but also something she could probably just go ahead and do.

I gave them my longlist, which I had, of course, populated in my head many times over but never told anyone: besides working in musicals, the holy grail, I would want to do brief stints in art, food, marine biology, and at Disney World (as a princess, ideally, but, given my age, more realistically as Cinderella's fairy godmother).

As the night (and drinks) went on, our ideas got more and more expansive: Zookeeper! Vegetable farmer! Zumba instructor! Park ranger! We were joking, but the more we talked about it, the more it was clear: what we all thirsted for, along with our forthcoming martinis, was change and adventure.

Once the weekend ended, talk of internships was firmly relegated to the "unattainable fantasy" category in my brain (alongside "move to Hawaii and open a shrimp shack on the beach" and "fit back into my jeans from high school"). In the light of day, the idea was almost laughable: Leave my job and children behind, forgo my place at the summit of the career mountain I had been scaling since college or before, and abandon my success for what? A chance to make coffee for strangers? There was no way. Relieving myself of my responsibilities was not in my DNA.

·········

Long, long ago, before lychee martinis were even a thing, I grew up your typical Cuban Jewish girl in a house that looked much like the others on a cul-de-sac in what was, at the time, the outlands of Miami. Any farther west of our little newly built subdivision and you hit the Everglades; you could smell the swamp from the driveway.

My dad had immigrated to the United States from Cuba in the 1960s like so many of his fellow exiles escaping Castro's iron grip. My mother grew up in a predominantly Jewish middle-class neighborhood in North Miami Beach. These two unlikely lovers met at a fraternity party at the University of Florida and she, two years older, pursued him for months before he finally agreed to a date. As a couple they never should have worked. He was a scrappy Catholic refugee who played drums in a band; she was a petite Jewish girl and a terrible cook, whose one attempt at baking was a disastrous recipe for lima bean cupcakes. But four years later, they got engaged and married very shortly after (yours truly arriving seven months later, fated to wonder for most of my childhood how I could have been born eight weeks premature, as my parents insisted, while also having weighed a healthy, hearty six pounds, two ounces).

Growing up we were far from poor, but we certainly weren't wealthy, which, based on my near-obsessive viewing of *Beverly Hills, 90210*, seemed like an enviable, if dramatic, thing to be; I didn't know any actual rich people to confirm the facts. As a kid, I was always hatching some moneymaking scheme—selling old books and toys, mixing Kool-Aid with lemonade and marking up the price by 300 percent—but never expanded my market share beyond my parents. Eventually I found a niche as a babysitter when I hit my preteen years, printing an advertisement on stationery meant for birth announcements ("It's a girl!"). My main selling points, emphasized in ALL CAPS, were that I was QUALIFIED and I had LOW RATE$$$. I charged $2.50 per hour. Once again, my only clients were my own parents, who paid me to watch my two younger brothers regularly and did not receive a friends-and-family discount.

When I was fourteen, our situation changed. My dad left the big accounting firm he was working at and set up his own business, which was going well. We moved to a bigger house in Coral Gables, a much fancier part of Miami, where streets with names like Madeira and Isla Dorada were denoted by low, white concrete markers meant to mimic natural limestone. My mom quit her job as a special education teacher to stay at home with my youngest brother, who was still in diapers. The faint smell of swamp was replaced by salty mangroves and expensive perfumes.

"So are we rich now?" I asked my dad.

"We're comfortable," he would say, never sharing more about his personal finances.

In spite of the fact that we had moved on up like the Jeffersons, our change in circumstances never meant a change in our work ethic. I was expected to fund my own desires, which I did from the age of fourteen. I held a part-time job at Books & Books, a local, beloved independent bookstore, where I conducted inventory in the children's room after school and on weekends and got early buzz on anticipated titles. ("Have you heard of this Harry Potter guy? He's going to be huge.") I also spent one misguided summer at the Dadeland Mall information booth, a job which required an unflattering uniform of boxy white polyester shirts, navy pants that buttoned four inches above the belly button, and a hideous scarf that needed to be tied jauntily around my neck at all times. It paid well but I ended up with bruised knees from ducking so often under the counter when friends walked by, lest I be seen.

When it came time to apply to colleges, there was only one place I truly wanted to go, the place all the hard work and straight A's had been leading to: Harvard. Never mind that I had never so much as set foot in New England or seen snow or thought critically about my course of study and whether Harvard was the right place for me. It had been on my vision board since age nine. Harvard was the best, and I always needed to be the best.

My dad agreed. He would pay for Harvard, he said, or University of Florida, where I knew I could get a full academic scholarship, but nothing in between. Princeton? HA! Yale? More like fail. It was Harvard or bust.

We were on vacation in New York, in line to see *Les Misérables*, when the neighbor who had been picking up our mail called to tell me I got accepted.

We were a musical-theater-obsessed family. My mother, like all nice Jewish girls, was a Barbra Streisand acolyte from a young age. Her parents loved musicals too, and my grandfather had even tried his hand at writing a few of his own, with limited success beyond the Temple Beth Torah audiences. (Surprisingly, his show *Isn't Everybody?*, about a team of monkey astronauts sent on a mission to Mars who arrived to discover that everyone there was Jewish, did not cross over to the mainstream.)

My dad's introduction to the genre came through my mom. On their first trip to New York, while they were dating and still in college, she took them to see *They're Playing Our Song*, a Neil Simon classic. My dad had always been a music lover, but the streets of Hialeah, Florida, rang out with disco and salsa, not Rodgers and Hammerstein. Nevertheless, he was instantly transfixed; he cried through the whole second act. Together my parents amassed a collection of cassette tapes of cast recordings to rival Lincoln Center's and raised my brothers and me on a steady diet of *Camelot* and *The Tap Dance Kid*.

The timing of that phone call telling me I had achieved my childhood goal could not have been more perfect: we loved musicals and we *loved* the idea of me going to Harvard—first generation born in the United States and already in the Ivy League. I was going to make something of my humble beginnings (much like Jean Valjean, but without the time on the chain gang). Education was the single biggest priority in our family, always had been—the immigrant's talisman to ward off the uncertainty of the future.

A few months after that night, I packed the contents of my life (like my dog-eared collection of Jane Austen novels and snakeskin pants in five different colors) into four suitcases and moved to the Cambridge side of the Charles River. Harvard was intimidating, but I more or less managed to stay afloat and, once I got the feeling back in my frostbitten fingers, even enjoyed it—immensely. I could not, however, figure out what was supposed to come next. I had spent so much time thinking about and planning for getting into Harvard that once I got there, it hadn't even occurred to me that I would one day have to leave and enter the real world.

I took a class called Behavioral Biology of Women my freshman year and was invited by the section leader—a graduate student—to a mixer for the women's studies department. The professors were warm and welcoming, the students fun and clever, and the snacks yummy—but what really sold me was the billing of the women's studies major as an "interdisciplinary degree," which meant I could take classes in any department. As long as they had something to do with gender, they would count for course credit. Deciding on a major that meant I didn't have to limit my horizons seemed perfect.

I called my dad the next day to tell him. "I chose a major," I shared with glee. "Women's studies."

It was quiet on the line for a good ten seconds.

"What is that?" he asked.

I gave him the spiel I had heard the night before, emphasizing the fact that I would get to take lots of different classes—"including economics," I threw in.

"And then afterward, you do what? Work at the women's studies factory?"

My dad had immigrated to Miami from Cuba at age eight, then worked night shifts at the airport all through high school to earn money. He had put himself through college with scholarships and loans, choosing accounting as his major, because that was what his older brother had done and it basically guaranteed a job upon graduation. It was that familiar, multigenerational, immigrant success story: my grandfather was a farmer so my father could be an accountant so I could wax poetic about Foucault and not shave my armpits.

I rolled my eyes over the phone. He didn't get it.

"Don't worry," I assured him. I don't think he believed me, but to his credit he pretended like he did.

Three years later, I found myself in London with a plan: find a job, study for a master's degree, or do absolutely anything I needed to in order to secure a visa so I could live there for as long as Her Majesty would allow. I was madly in love with the UK, an Anglophile of epic proportions. I blame Richard Curtis. I watched *Bridget Jones's Diary*, *Love Actually*, and my personal favorite, *Notting Hill* (a film I have seen so many times I could repeat all of the dialogue verbatim, on cue), over and over again. In those movies I saw my future: me sitting at a table in a bistro on a leafy West London street or crossing Tower Bridge in a power suit on the way to work.

My way into the country was a master's program at the London School of Economics and Political Science in gender studies. I could study in London. My dad begrudgingly agreed that an advanced degree was acceptable (even if it was in gender studies). And the program came with a student visa. The UK was so different from anything I had ever known, and it was exciting. In London, I was the exotic one. There was no backstory, no clear road laid out ahead. In this space, an ocean away from everyone who knew me, I was master of my own story. I was free and unencumbered.

But within a few years, I was working at a business strategy consulting firm (I still didn't know what we really did) and deeply in love with Carlos Miranda, whose grandparents had been neighbors with my own grandparents in Cuba. Growing up, I had never met Carlos, who was raised mostly outside of the United States, but I knew his grandmother, who lived near my own in Miami, very well. Martha had been a fixture in my own childhood, so when she emailed both me and her grandson, who was also coming to study in London for a year, I knew I had to comply with whatever she requested:

From: Abuela Martha
To: Alisha and Carlos
Date: August 16, 2004

Carli and Alisha,

I am sending you both your addresses. Alisha, my grandson's name is Carlos Miranda, and Carli, her name is as it shows on her address. I really hope you can get to be friends; your respective fathers are also the same age and have been friends forever.

Love you both, Martha

The two of us started having Wagamama Mondays, regular Japanese lunches where we used two-for-one coupons we cut out from a magazine we got at student orientation. When he offered me the last dumpling, I knew we were both smitten.

Getting into a serious relationship at twenty-two was not in the life plan I had written out for myself. But he was my soul mate, and we were immediately a unit. We moved to New York together (his idea, not mine, but I was on board) and took up residence in a fifth-floor walk-up in Manhattan where the bathroom and kitchen were the same room.

A series of power jobs followed, first in New York and then in London, when I finally convinced Carlos to marry me and the Queen and her very nice immigration officials to let us back in. Those jobs carried me through the next fifteen years. Each was interesting and paid well. Each provided me with something I needed at the moment: more money, a better title, new skills, the chance to manage a team. But in time, they became tedious and repetitive, or I outgrew the position.

In the meantime, I had children, my twins, Theo and Lola. Balancing work and motherhood became a constant struggle. My entire life was a rush of code-switching: spooning oatmeal into mouths in the morning, trying to be a boss and manager all day long, being home in time for bath and lullabies in the evening, then going back to emails and firefighting until I could pass out in my own bed and do it all again the next day. So in 2011, when Carlos decided to set up his own business and asked me to join him, I jumped at the chance. Under the stipulation that he could never, ever tell me what to do.

Our company, I.G. Advisors, is a consulting firm in the social impact space, a jargony way of saying that it helps connect companies and foundations with charitable organizations (think a diaper company funding UNICEF). The business grew and thrived, and after a couple of years, I took over as CEO.

At last, I "had it all": an expanding business, a family, my dream life in London. And I thought I was happy. I told everyone I was happy. But over time, like a boulder slowly eroding as it's crashed upon by waves until it's no more than a pebble, I came to realize that I really, really wasn't.

Work plus life had gradually become so intense that some mornings I thought about the sheer number of tasks required to keep the business and family afloat that day and fantasized about getting back into bed, burrowing into one of the air pockets deep under the duvet, and doing nothing but watching season 4 of *Gilmore Girls* on repeat for the rest of my life. I would start trying to practically assess my chance of getting Carlos to install an IV drip for sustenance next to my bed, before I would realize that of course I couldn't do that. I had to get up, respond to emails, deal with HR issues, meet with clients to sell them some business, solve their problems, pick up the kids, make a stupid piece of macaroni art, cook dinner, and then do it all again the next day.

I had overcommitted but told myself that maybe if I still loved my job—really loved it, like I once did way back in my twenties and even my early thirties, when I found the pressure exhilarating and got a buzz from making a sale or a warm glow from a client's praise—I wouldn't feel so awful. But I didn't, and it was tough to admit, especially since I had spent so long working toward this one point. Making some sort of major pivot would seem like I had wasted time when I should have been doing something else.

What else? I didn't know. But really, maybe anything else. I had fallen into a life that was not what I wanted and I couldn't see any way to escape from it without tossing a live grenade into the carefully constructed world I had built for myself and my family. I loved my husband and my children and they loved their lives. They were happy, even if I wasn't. I couldn't just uproot everyone to move to Mumbai for a year to pursue my lifelong dream of Bollywood stardom, or transfer us all to Tokyo while I made a case for casting me as Ariel on the Disney parade route. Not without making everyone miserable, decimating our family finances, and jacking up the kids' future therapy bills to astronomical heights.

I was stuck.

One more thought haunted me, a deep and dark one that came unwelcome in the hopeless hours just before sunrise when you're sure the day will never come. I was careening toward forty, and I was terrified of becoming what I had always feared since the first time I saw *American Beauty* as an impressionable seventeen year old: a sad, miserable, crying-in-the-shower middle-aged woman whose best years were behind her and who spent all her time dreaming about the what-ifs of her past and wishing, desperately, that she had chased them down. If I didn't do something now, she would be me. I was already crying into my coffee. I was halfway there.

Over and over, I heard the same tiny question in my head: Is this it? It wasn't that I didn't have enough or even that I didn't have everything I wanted. The problem was that I *did* have everything I wanted—or that I had thought I wanted, that I had worked toward so arduously and for so long. Everything that everyone I respected in my life—especially my parents and grandparents before me—had hoped I would have.

 But what if this was all I was ever going to achieve? Was I finished trying new things, having new experiences, getting those butterflies in my tummy when I was nervous about pushing my own boundaries? I worried that I had made all the big decisions I was going to make, took the big risks, and that everything was going to be the same from here on out.

As soon as I allowed myself to spiral down that rabbit hole of misery, I immediately felt painfully and viscerally guilty. Poor, privileged, spoiled brat, miserable because she got what she wanted and now she wants more. How dare I? After everything that had been sacrificed for me to get where I was,

I deigned to want something different. I felt awful, and then felt awful for feeling awful.

As consultant, as a CEO, as a mom, it had been my job to fix everything, manage everything, organize everything, and present a solution. But here I was with a problem I couldn't solve. And the fear—the cold, gripping terror that I would never be able to solve it, that I would always feel unhappy, that my days of challenges and excitement at the prospect of waking up in the morning to start a new day were over—was real and ever present.

I didn't hate my job. My job was empirically very cool. I was essentially giving away other people's money to good causes. I liked my volunteer roles, supporting nonprofits that helped a lot of people. I loved my husband and my kids and planning pancake breakfasts for my fellow school moms. Each thing on its own was fine. But the combination felt crushing.

Maybe I couldn't chase Bollywood stardom or become a Disney princess for the long term. But I could do that—or something like it—for a month at a time. A short vacation from my job, a small hiatus from my real life.

An internship.

The morning after my night with Laura and Rebecca at the Coral Room, we dragged ourselves out of bed and downstairs for breakfast in pajamas and sweatpants. We were hungover and in need of caffeine, but the effect of the child-free buzz we had been feeling all weekend was still there. With our plates piled high with yogurt and granola and eggs and toast, we sat in companionable silence. I was still thinking about our conversation the night before.

"So this internship thing," Laura said. "I think you should do it. You can talk to my dad about it." Laura's dad, John Weidman, is a legendary theater writer, whose pen was behind

Broadway hits like *Contact, Assassins,* and *Pacific Overtures.*
He had known me for a long time, since Laura and I shared a
room with Rebecca and seven other girls in college and were
so feral that we once left a birthday cake under the sofa, only
to find it four months later. It still took us two weeks to throw
it out. "I'm sure he could help you find something."

I felt my heart skip a beat before it fell back into its normal
rhythm. Could this really be a thing?

"I agree," said Rebecca. "And you should write a book
about it when you're done."

I looked down at my now lukewarm cappuccino. Become
a professional writer. Now, that seemed even more far-fetched
than a Broadway internship. But what if? It had been a long,
long time since I'd let myself indulge in something as distract-
ing—and as magical—as a "what if?"

That's probably why I kept coming back to the idea over
and over again, circling around it so much; it had emerged
in my mind less as "fantasy" and more and more as "simple
solution to every single one of my emotional crises." It pre-
sented a way out, at least for a little while. If I just moved
this around in my calendar or turned down that client, maybe
there was a way to make it work.

Every morning at three, I woke to my brain playing Ping-
Pong with itself. I found myself drafting imaginary emails to
contacts in the art world or thinking about how I might tailor
my résumé for a job at a hotel. But then, in the clear light of the
morning, reality would set in. Fear and reality. I had too many
obligations, too many responsibilities, too many things other
people needed from me; I couldn't see any fathomable way to
bridge the gulf that seemed to exist between idea and internship.

While on vacation, things came to a head. I was supposed
to be enjoying time off from work with my husband and

children but instead found myself waking up each morning listening to the birds as tears streamed from my eyes. I knew I couldn't continue pretending that everything was fine for much longer, but I felt stuck.

At last, Carlos came to the rescue. "What *is* stopping you?" he asked. "Quit whining and just do it."

"How?" I asked, bereft. "How would I even get started?"

"Just take one step. Pick a month, block it off right now in your calendar, and work toward getting your first internship. We'll figure the other stuff out later."

He was right (don't tell him I said that). I had always been, if nothing else, a girl who loves a plan. Thinking about all the steps at once was overwhelming and terrifying, but just taking the next step was simple enough. I immediately pulled up my work calendar. I scrolled ahead to the first empty weeks I could find—still a good six months away—and I blocked off an entire month with the suitably vague but firm "Alisha Out of the Office." February 2020 felt like a lifetime away, but at least it was a start.

Somehow, just knowing that "Out of Office" was in my calendar was the thing I needed to take the next step: actually finding an internship. Broadway was the dream—and I had a solid connection—but the more I thought seriously about some of the other jobs I'd considered before, like in art and marine biology, the wider my search became. I tackled the task with my signature gusto and borderline unhealthy Excel obsession, creating an "internship relationship management" spreadsheet. One row at a time, I populated the list with my hopes and dreams alongside details of people I pulled off of LinkedIn. I included former coworkers, passing acquaintances from college, friends' cousins (and their dads), and exes and their new partners. I was not picky. Anyone who could help me get my foot in the door made it onto the list.

Emotionally and practically it was one step forward and forty steps back. I'd get nervous and say I was too busy to keep working on this dumb idea anyway and push it to the side for a week before coming back to it in the middle of the night as if it were the only thing that was going to save me. I would delete the "Alisha Out of Office" in my calendar, only to put it back in a few minutes later. But then I'd do something real, like draft an email to send to all of these random contacts and their relatives, something that would convince them that my email account had not been hacked but that I really, really wanted to be their intern. Then I would redraft it sixteen times, eventually, coming up with something that didn't make me want to vomit:

> Thank you in advance for taking the time to read this conventional request (an unpaid internship) from an unconventional candidate. I'm undertaking a personal project, exploring the career paths I almost chased—but, due to circumstance, chance, and choice, did not—by taking on a series of internships and documenting them. Fifteen years into my professional life, my aim is to gain a deeper understanding of what the X industry is truly like, as a way to better inform the next 15 years. As such, I'm hoping you will consider allowing me to undertake a four-week, unpaid internship at Y.

The polished draft felt real and legit, so even though I still questioned my own sanity regularly, I willed myself to continue the search, executing on all of my professional action verbs: Networking! Emailing! Cold calling! Social media stalking!

The other element of this plan that kept stopping me in my tracks was figuring out how I was going to create not just the time but the space—physically, mentally, and emotionally—to explore this new path. Taking on an internship, even for a few

weeks, was going to require me to extricate myself from some
of my existing responsibilities, which, in recent years, had
ballooned to encompass maybe three people's full-time jobs,
as somewhere along the line I had come to equate being busy
with being happy. In addition to running my own company, I
had built and launched a sustainable-fashion app a few years
before that I was trying to expand, plus I volunteered on the
board of three nonprofit organizations and the school parent council. And then of course there was the mental load of
managing the family: grocery shopping and planning meals,
liaising with our nanny and other babysitters to make sure
we had childcare always in place; acting as a travel agent for
family vacations; booking appointments for the vet, dentist,
doctor, or physiotherapist; scheduling playdates; baking cakes
for the bake sales; and more or less saying yes to anything
anyone asked me to do. All because I could not say no.

In my head, I had a vision of myself as a straight-talking,
straight-shooting badass: Sandy at the end of *Grease*. But actually, all Sandy was, underneath the perm and the black leggings
and the cigarette, was her same old self with a makeover: a
cheerleading, ponytail-swishing, people pleaser. And so was I.

No one had ever explicitly said to me, "It's your job to
never, ever let anyone down," but I felt it innately anyway.
Maybe it was being the oldest child, or being a girl, or just
the sheer fact that I was competent and good at stuff from
an early age so I was praised for that, and that praise sure
felt good. But whatever the reason, I always felt compelled to
make everyone happy.

Eighteen years ago, when I got engaged, a former boss gave
a toast in my honor. He raised his glass and told the whole
company that I was a model employee—and that what made
me this way, he was certain, was that I never, ever wanted

to disappoint my parents. It was entirely true. I have never liked to disappoint people, definitely not my parents, Alex and Mindy, but also not my teachers or bosses, and don't even get me started on my husband, my kids, my friends. I was an aggressive people pleaser. Look at me, I'm Sandra Dee.

Making space for the internships meant that I would have to disappoint some people, which made me even more nauseated than contemplating drafting a résumé with photos on it. But I knew I had to channel my inner Rizzo and start stepping back from some of my many obligations. It was far from easy, but I had become so fixated on the internships, the plan, the resolution to all my inner turmoil and tears, that I was at a breaking point. Disappointing people was bad, but disappointing myself seemed, all of a sudden, to be truly unbearable.

I would love to tell you that I boldly marched into each and every office, slammed the notice of my resignation down on the table, and walked out again before they had time to try and change my mind. I didn't. I tried. And I failed. When I told the headmistress of my kids' school I was going to step aside from the parent council, she asked me to stay. "Just one more school year," she pleaded. I caved.

But a few weeks later, I delicately began untangling myself by noting that it was temporary. "I'm taking a series of mini-sabbaticals," I said cheerfully. "I'll definitely be back."

Or at least that is what I kept telling myself and everyone else. "Midlife crisis," I'd say, winking. "It's my *Eat Pray Love*. Carlos just better hope I don't leave him for a surfer in Bali." I joked and made light of the decision, and perhaps I really believed that at the time. The premise of the internships seemed exciting enough to shake me out of whatever was bothering me but not too drastic. I would just take a little break from all my worries and obligations and, most important, my job. I would sow my wild professional oats and come back, refreshed and ready to return to the life I had worked so hard to build.

I had to believe that, because the alternative was frightening. Sure, it was fun to fantasize about having a completely different career, a life that was unrecognizable from the one I had at the moment. But in the harsh light of day, I didn't see any permanent off-ramps from the path I had set on so many years before. I craved change, the way I craved Pop-Tarts and won ton soup when I was pregnant (viscerally and all the time); I desired the freedom of newness; I wanted to feel that delightful terror of the unknown. But it seemed absurd. So, what, I would just throw away decades of accomplishments and achievements that brought me to the C-suite? I'd risk my comfortable financial situation and steady schedule that suited my maternal obligations?

Nope, that was something that other people did. Less responsible people, perhaps, or those with less to lose. I couldn't fathom doing something so irrational. The internships—mini-sabbaticals, tiny breaks, whatever I wanted to call this—would be enough. I just needed a vacation from real life; then I'd feel recharged and everything would go back to normal.

So I continued whittling away at my list of to-dos and steps back and steps down. Eventually, I silenced the voice inside of me screaming "YES! OKAY! I'LL DO IT! JUST PLEASE LIKE ME!" for long enough to create a relatively clear calendar in front of me, for the first time in a long time. Now all I had to do was find an internship to fill it with. The hard part was over, and the offers started pouring in.

Just kidding. Actually, nothing happened. Most of my emails weren't even acknowledged, and those who did respond rejected my offer outright. It was surprising how difficult it was to convince people to let me work for them for free, with no strings attached.

I kept on pounding the digital and physical pavement, sending hundreds of emails begging for an informational coffee to explain my pitch in person and scrolling through social media for tenuous connections to anyone remotely connected in any way to my industries of choice. Besides Broadway, I kept coming up with more fields I thought I should explore. Art was a big one—it had always been an interest of mine, and I fantasized about working on the curatorial team at a big museum. In high school I thought I wanted to be a marine zoologist, feeding seals and teaching them to clap. I wondered about fashion, especially sustainable fashion, and working for a designer. The possibilities were endless.

I had a couple of interviews in cool industries in which I would have loved to intern (and even some in which I did not, but I wasn't going to be picky) set up for me by friends, or friends of friends or very distant acquaintances, but most of them just wanted free advice about philanthropy—the thing I had been doing for fifteen years. It was discouraging.

Fortunately, I was not a person who was easily discouraged. I got into Harvard but had applied to a bunch of other schools in case I wasn't accepted. I made sure I never had less than two dozen rolls of toilet paper in my house so I would never be left high and (not) dry. I knew that everything was a numbers game. Once I got one internship, the next would follow. All I had to do was keep calm and carry on, shoot off another five emails, friend another ten people on LinkedIn, and something would happen. I'd be on Broadway before you could say 525,600 minutes, and then who knows what would come next.

Chapter 2
Overture

Stephen Sondheim's *Company* is still, to this day, one of the most insightful musicals ever mounted about heterosexual marriage, even though it was written by a single, closeted gay man in 1970. *Company* follows Bobby, a thirty-five-year-old bachelor, assiduously avoiding marriage like the plague. Good old Bobby watches his friends navigate their own relationships with varying degrees of unhappiness and spends most of the musical terrified by the idea of commitment.

The music is still incredible, but the old "can't tie a fella down" trope has gotten a bit stale, so in 2018, Marianne Elliott mounted a revival that gender-swapped all of the roles. It was a fresh take on a classic. Bobby becomes Bobbie, a single woman in her thirties who fervently does not want anyone to put a ring on it. She flits through a stream of handsome gentlemen callers, enjoying nights of passion without days of responsibility.

In one scene, set to an instrumental song called "Tick Tock," Bobbie has a feverish nightmare that she's married, spending her days literally barefoot and pregnant, toting a laundry basket that never seems to empty from room to room. She wakes up relieved that it was only a dream. When she imagines what others might consider "domestic bliss," it's with abject terror.

As my taxi entered the Midtown tunnel, Manhattan's gleaming skyline in the distance, I thought about Bobbie and her far wiser life choices. My cell phone lost service, cutting off my husband midsentence. Carlos had been repeating back to me my instructions on how to use the washing machine, something he had never done before, and asking my advice on the best setting for cleaning Lola's stuffed bunny, which was currently covered in vomit.

Domestic bliss, babe.

My day had started about twenty hours earlier, in my kitchen in London, where I sat around the table with Carlos and the kids for our last breakfast before I would leave for New York and what I was now calling the next phase of my life (no pressure). It was February, Leap Day, which felt appropriate since I was leaping into the unknown.

I was saying goodbye for two weeks. After that, the three of them would fly to New York to meet me, and I'd finish out my internship with my family in tow. The emotions around the table were mixed. The twins were upset, especially Lola, who was trying not to cry. I kept a bright smile on my face, as did Carlos. "This is mommy's big adventure," he told them. "We are so excited for her."

"But I'm going to miss you," Lola replied.

"I know, my love, but you'll see me in just two short weeks. You will barely notice I'm gone."

I did not think that was true, but I was already feeling guilty as hell, so I was saying it for my own benefit as much as hers.

Carlos, for his part, was doing an amazing job of encouraging me in spite of the fact that I know he was terrified that I was leaving. He would, of course, never admit this. His constant refrain if I expressed any concern in the weeks leading up to my departure was "everything will be fine." In the years past, I had taken short trips for work or play, and everything had always *ended up* fine (barring one broken arm). But by the second day of each of those trips, I could hear the frustration in his voice at the challenges of being a single parent. Each time I returned, he would give me a welcome-back hug and kiss and then lock himself in his man cave for the next twenty-four hours to decompress before reemerging a new man. Fortunately for me, Carlos is blessed with rose-colored hindsight, so he never hesitates to agree to the next time, having conveniently forgotten what transpired before.

And then there was an unexpected hitch in the plan: a thing called coronavirus that everyone in London was still making jokes about, as if it was something you got after drinking one too many Mexican beers. But the truth was the BBC was running story after story. The night before, we had sat together on the sofa, legs entangled, making an apocalypse plan that I, for my part, was sure we would never have to use. The virus seemed to have been contained to China, Iran, and Italy. There were few cases in the UK and no one seemed unduly panicked. Except for Carlos, who was convinced the end was nigh.

We decided that if things got bad—although we really had no idea what "bad" was going to entail—he would take the kids up to our house in rural Scotland and I would fly back and meet them there. I had bought four crazy-looking gas masks before I left, the kind that make you look like an alien from a 1960s sci-fi film, and he would pack those, along with other essentials (passports, coffee beans) in a "go bag."

We were quiet for a few moments, each considering what could come to pass in the weeks ahead. I knew I had to say it, but I didn't want to say it. I really didn't want to say it. But my guilt won out.

"I can stay," I said, not really meaning it. "I don't have to go."

I held my breath as I waited for his response. Because the truth was that I really did have to go. I had pushed it all down, the fear and guilt, because I felt like there was something worse than a respiratory virus awaiting me if I stayed behind.

"Of course you have to go," he said. I sighed deeply, my relief palpable. I had convinced myself everything was going to be fine and needed his reassurance to believe that it would be. He was unconvinced but hid it as well as he could.

After breakfast several hours later, with fewer tears than I had expected, I said goodbye and raced to Heathrow Airport, where, after a few intimate moments with a security guard who patted me down, I was sitting on the plane and genuinely feeling, for the first time in a long time, like nothing could go wrong.

Once upon a time, I was terrified of flying. My coping mechanism was to get fall-down drunk before takeoff, but eventually even that failed to take the edge off, so I upgraded to popping a (prescribed) Xanax to survive the flight. My fear miraculously subsided once I had children and flying alone became a decadent luxury, my peaceful escape. For however many hours I was in the air, no one could call me or contact me as I ate candy I wasn't hungry for, watched bad movies I would never have paid to see in the theater (even if I had the time to go to the movie theater anymore, which I did not), and brainlessly paged through the tawdriest gossip magazines on the market. It was awesome.

While half listening to *Mamma Mia 2* and flipping through *People*, assessing the evidence as to whether Jennifer Aniston did or did not have lip fillers, it dawned on me that these few weeks alone would be the longest I had ever been on my own in my entire life. I went from living with my parents as a child to living with roommates in college and grad school; moving in with my then boyfriend, later husband, at twenty-three; and never looking back. This brief period was going to be the most independent I had been in years—since the last time I left everything behind to escape my life.

This feeling I had been feeling, the irrepressible sense that things were out of my control, had happened to me once before, during my junior year of college. Looking back, it's almost laughable how low the stakes were back then—my worries were about disappointing my a cappella group or knocking a few tenths of a point off my GPA—but that feeling of a black cloud looming over me 24/7 was no joke.

My roommate accompanied me to the campus health center. I walked into the therapist's office and cried for forty-five straight minutes. When I left, blowing my nose into a discarded tissue I found in my coat pocket, I felt slightly better. I had a plan.

"I need to get out of here," I told my parents over the phone. Winter in Cambridge was setting in and it was dark outside at just five thirty. I pictured them huddled over the speakerphone in their living room in Miami, where the sun was still shining.

"What does that mean?" they asked.

"I'll go study abroad," I responded, glad to share my newfound clarity. "That way I don't lose a semester, I'll graduate on time, and I can, you know, just get away from everything for a while."

"I don't think that's a good idea," I heard my dad say. "You can't run away from your problems."

"Well, I can't stay here," I said. "Either I study abroad or I take the semester off. But I need to do something different or I don't know what will happen."

Although I had a well-documented flair for the dramatic, they knew me. They heard the desperation in my voice and acquiesced, agreeing to fund a semester abroad. I applied at the last minute to a program in London, where I spent six months wandering around ancient corners and taking week-end trips to Edinburgh and Dublin on my own, doing only what I wanted, whenever I wanted to. I worked part-time at a busy pub and went dancing every weekend and kissed boys I shouldn't have and took the night bus, picking up a ham-burger made of questionable animal meat on the way home (it was the smell of grilling onions; gets me every time).

When I came home at the end of the summer, the black cloud was gone. I was able to breathe easier and focus on my final year, and the future beyond it, with optimism. Just know-ing that I had the freedom to pack up and leave everything behind for a short period of time, clear my head, and know that the world would not fall apart gave me the confidence to say no to things like taking on extra work for classes that I didn't need to do or going to parties I didn't feel like attending.

But twenty years later, I was back here again: feeling like my obligations were clawing at me and desperate to run away. This was my grown-up version of a semester abroad. A temporary escape. I would be able to make plans without worrying about anyone's needs but my own. I could go out, unconcerned if a babysitter was available. More than that, I could just *go out* if I felt like it. Without any advance planning whatsoever. I could order Ethiopian food for takeout and no one would complain they'd prefer Chinese; I could wash dishes in my undies or, better yet, not wash them at all. For a brief period of time, the only person I had to answer to was me. I could park my obligations in short-term and come back for them in a few weeks. The thought was electrifying.

It was also an illusion. Because, even at thirty-six thousand feet in the air, I really didn't get to leave my obligations and responsibilities behind for long. Reality came crashing back down as soon as the plane had landed and my phone slid back into service.

I pinged off a customary text to my husband: *Landed [smiley face emoji, American flag emoji]*. I could see the two blue checkmarks indicating that it had been read—surprising, given that it was well after midnight in the UK—but no response was being typed. Odd.

I called to check in and the moment he picked up the call, I knew something was wrong by the tone of his voice.

"Hey."

"What's wrong?" I said, my mind immediately flying to the possibilities both mundane and far-fetched, but all of them terrible.

It was quiet on the line.

"What happened?" I pushed, now starting to get frantic and convinced some sort of hostage scenario starring Liam Neeson was unfolding at my house.

"Everyone's okay," he said. Relief swept over me. "But about fifteen minutes ago both of the kids started projectile vomiting. I think it's food poisoning. One made it to the toilet but the other threw up all over the bedroom. I really have to go. Where's the laundry detergent? I'll call you back."

We spoke again both before and after the Midtown tunnel, so he could point the camera at the washing machine and ask which dial to turn. Finally, once the laundry was sudsing and the kids were fast asleep, we hung up the phone, both exhausted.

After we said goodbye, I rolled down the taxi window, feeling a little nauseated myself after all that talk of vomit, and stared outside at the city around me. It was a Saturday night and the streets of Manhattan were bustling. Groups of girls in too-short skirts and too-tall heels tried to wave down my cab, hoping it was empty and looking disappointed when it passed them by. That was me once upon a New York night, but it had been a long time since I had let my legs be exposed to the February air in that way. I was too old and too sensible for that anymore.

I was feeling guilty and a little bit delirious, but as we made our way downtown and into the West Village, the nausea subsided and excitement took its place. I had done it. I was here!

I had found the apartment on Airbnb just a few days earlier after so many internet searches that I nearly lost the will to live. My requirements were not, I thought, unreasonable: a one-bedroom, so when Carlos came with the kids in a few weeks we could all be comfortable and not crammed into a studio; not ridiculously expensive—this was an unpaid internship, after all; and walking distance to the Classic Stage Company's theater premises on East Thirteenth Street, where I assumed rehearsals would be taking place.

When I finally spotted a West Village "gem" with lots of "natural light" that sat just above a "fine dining restaurant," I clicked "book" right away. It was just a six-minute walk to the theater to boot. Housing secured, there was nothing to worry about. Unlike my other attempts at an internship, the Broadway one came together so easily. Mostly due to the kindness of others.

Laura's dad, John Weidman, had completely come through for me. When I emailed him about my idea—to intern at a musical—he offered to introduce me to his friends. Within hours, he had sent two emails. The first was to John Doyle, the Scottish-born, globally revered director whose brain was behind Tony-winning revivals such as 2005's *Sweeney Todd* and 2006's (non-gender-bent) *Company*. John Doyle was mounting a revival of *Assassins*, a show written by none other than John Weidman himself along with Stephen Sondheim, at the off-Broadway Classic Stage Company.

His second email went to James Lapine, a writer and director known for Broadway hits *Falsettos, Sunday in the Park with George*, and *Passion*. James had written and directed a brand-new show for the larger, Broadway theater at Lincoln Center. John Weidman described it to me thus: "It's called *Flying Over Sunset* and it's about Aldous Huxley, Clare Boothe Luce, and Cary Grant, all of whom took LSD. I'm not making this up."

When I saw the emails, I screamed. And showed Carlos.

"Who are these guys?" he asked.

I tried to put it into language he would understand: a niche star who was revered by a tiny subset of devotees as a god. "It's like if you were introduced to Jonathan Frakes," I said, referring to the actor who played Commander Riker in *Star Trek: The Next Generation.*

He understood immediately.

I wrote a short reply to both directors but ran it by John Weidman, who advised me not to assume that these seasoned professionals needed any extra help—"They've both done this a lot and I'm sure they've got their bases covered"—and suggested I remind them the more specific ways I might be useful. "You're smart, quick, and you're not a kid," he said. "It's probably worth telling them that you'd be up for anything."

His final warning: "One thing you don't want to do is sound like a tourist. Someone who wants a month off from her 'real life' to take one of those overpriced Harvard Alumni Tours to Patagonia and Antarctica, or in this case to Musical Theater."

A month off from my real life was exactly what I wanted, but I kept that to myself. I was far from a tourist—for one thing, when I'm an actual tourist, I never wake up before nine, don't do more than one activity per day, and definitely don't get coffee for anyone but myself.

I wanted to work; I was desperate to work, actually. Especially on Broadway. Not only did I want to see if there could be a job for me within the theater, but I needed to justify to myself the extended time away from my career and my family.

Both directors wrote back quickly and were open and welcoming. James asked if I could read music. "No, but I could learn!" I replied, not at all confident that I could. He told me that there weren't any actual jobs to offer but that *Flying Over Sunset* would be in "tech" and I was welcome to come and observe. I had no idea what "tech" was. I said yes immediately.

John Doyle's production of *Assassins* would start rehearsing at the beginning of March in preparation for an April opening. He wasn't sure what there would be for me to do, but I was welcome there too. "Consider the Classic Stage Company your home for the month," he warmly replied.

My taxi pulled up to my Airbnb, a red-brick prewar building on a West Village street. I thanked the driver as he pulled my heavy suitcases out of the trunk. They were filled with everything I thought I would need for a month in New York as a theater intern, but the truth was I didn't have a clue. What did people wear to rehearsals? Business casual? Or maybe sort of kooky creative vintage numbers that they had hand-sewn themselves using old Popsicle sticks instead of zippers?

Asking was too embarrassing, so I packed whatever I could think of. Blazers and jeans, heeled boots, nice flats, a formal gown (in case I needed to dress up for an opening night), thermal underwear, and, inexplicably for March in New York City, a bathing suit.

Also weighing down my bag: *The Secret Life of the American Musical* by Jack Viertel, *The Business of Broadway* by Mitch Weiss and Perri Gaffney, and of course, a printed and bound libretto of *Assassins*, which had quickly become my most prized possession. It contained all the lines, music, and lyrics of the show, and I had pored over it in the weeks leading up to my trip and all through the flight.

Shortly after ringing the bell, I was buzzed in and lugged my bags upstairs. The door opened. A curly-haired man, a few years younger, greeted me, as did the overwhelming smell of marijuana and a thumping bass line. "Hey," he drawled. "Welcome to your home for the next few weeks."

The chorus of "Billie Jean" wafted through the floorboards as clearly as if I were on the dance floor myself. Six white-noise machines strategically dotting the apartment whirled in tandem. All warning signs pointed to the fact that this rental was going to be as far from a quiet respite as I was from my husband and children back at home. But I was tired, jet-lagged, and determined to let nothing stand in the way of my dream. I rushed the guy out the door with a hasty promise to water all the plants, dreams of a deep and peaceful slumber ahead of me. Once the music shut off. If the music ever shut off.

The "fine dining restaurant" downstairs was actually a Philly Cheesesteak Kitchen ("kitchen" was generous), which was actually just a dive bar with, I could only assume, patrons who had early-onset hearing loss. I turned on the white-noise machines—all of them—popped some industrial-grade earplugs into my ears, and lay down, feeling the music pulsing inside my skull.

As "Livin' on a Prayer" blared beneath me, I stared at the ceiling and questioned whether the predicament in which I had landed myself was truly the doorway to my new life. I was an ocean away from an overwhelmed husband and two sick children, who lay huddled up in my bed (their own room reeked of vomit for a week after and required a team of professional cleaners to finally rid it of the smell), wishing their wife and mother was there to comfort them. I had left my comfortable Tempur-Pedic mattress and two layers of blackout curtains in London for a lumpy bed in a tiny NYC apartment with music so ear-piercingly loud that it was positively going to ruin Bon Jovi for me forever.

But it was worth it—tomorrow I'd be backstage on Broadway.

......

Before this project was even a project, before I had even drunkenly pitched the skeleton concept to Laura and Rebecca, when it was an unformed idea rolling around in my brain like a mound of Play-Doh, I knew that working in musical theater had to be one of my internships. The suburbs of Miami are a long way from Times Square, but I have loved musicals for as long as I can remember loving anything.

While other toddlers were singing "Twinkle, Twinkle, Little Star," I knew all the words to *Dreamgirls*. I could reel off stats on Tony Awards and collected *Playbill*s like baseball cards. My childhood bedroom is covered with posters of shows whose cast albums I listened to so many times that I intimately knew the places where each CD was scratched. I was to musicals what my husband is to *Star Trek*: obsessed, knowledgeable, passionate, and full of obstinate, annoying opinions (I'm sorry, but *Natasha, Pierre & the Great Comet of 1812* was totally overrated).

As a child, I was a pint-sized drama queen, which, combined with a tendency to be very bossy, meant my family was often held hostage to my theatrical whims. By eight, I was the self-appointed director, writer, producer, and emcee of our annual family Christmas shows. I was exacting and ruthless, with a typed script with the patter written in. ("Thank you, Matt Ross, all the way from the Peach State, for that soulful rendition of 'Silent Night.' It brought tears to my eyes.") No one was permitted, under any circumstances, to deviate from my script. My cousin Katie, always a rebel, loved to ad-lib. I retaliated by cutting her solo and relegating her to obscurity as "ten pipers piping" in the group sing-along of "The Twelve Days of Christmas." (Or is it "eleven pipers piping"? You see what I mean? No one cares about the pipers.)

While I loved the stage, I never followed the yellow brick road to musical stardom or even to musical obscurity. I sang in the chorus in middle school but abandoned it once puberty hit. The pecking order in high school was clear: athletes and cheerleaders were at the top of the pyramid. I had to be on top of the pyramid. Literally. I made JV cheer my first year, then varsity, and eventually became captain of my squad.

None of which stopped me from desperately wanting to be onstage every time there was a school musical, but I kept those desires to myself, knowing full well it would be social suicide.

In college, it was a different ball game altogether. At my small public high school in Miami, I had always felt that trying out for something—a show or concert or choir—was just a matter of raising your hand. I'd make it in. Everybody made it in. But my fellow Harvard students were overwhelming—a different species of human being. A girl I met doing a keg stand at a party was a concert pianist and had played at Carnegie Hall. I auditioned for a volunteer dance company whose members included Natalie Portman and was rejected (for a volunteer job!). I had been editor in chief of my school newspaper, but when I went to a meet-and-greet at the *Crimson*, where everyone else's parents seemed to be buddy-buddy with *New Yorker* writers (I had not at that point even ever seen an issue of *The New Yorker*), I left before the cheese plate was even half-empty.

I adjusted to my new role as "medium-sized fish in enormous ocean" by sticking to my strengths, the stuff that had gotten me into Harvard: a perfect score on my AP calculus exam, a 4.0 GPA, and a deep obsession with never missing a deadline for an assignment. I still dreamed of performance or creative pursuits and did end up eventually joining an a cappella group and, in my last year, taking a dubious turn as "Hot Box Girl No. 2" in our dorm production of *Guys and Dolls*, but I buried all my dreams of turning a life in the theater into a paying gig deep underneath academic achievement bullet points on my résumé.

I saw student productions of classic musicals like *Into the Woods* (my first exposure to James Lapine) and *Thoroughly Modern Millie* three or four times. I watched Drew Barrymore get crowned the Hasty Pudding Woman of the Year. I even went to plays (*without music*). But as I looked longingly at flyers advertising new shows, I resigned myself to sitting in the audience. While I had a decent singing voice, I didn't think I was good enough to "make it." But the question had always lingered: What would it really be like? Every time I listened to the soundtrack of a new musical, or every time I bought a ticket to one of Andrew Lloyd Webber's many productions in London or New York (some of which I adored—*Jesus Christ*

Superstar—and others that were two and a half hours of my life I would never get back—I'm looking at you, *The Woman in White*), I thought about what might have been.

My lack of any real experience meant that I knew very little about what a career in musical theater would actually entail. I had some idea about what it meant to be a producer or director, but it had been mostly gleaned from *The Producers* (it seemed to involve swindling elderly ladies). In the weeks preceding my start dates at *Assassins* and *Flying Over Sunset*, I even let myself fantasize a little. Sure, this was just supposed to be a minisabbatical—but what if I really did have the chops to make it, at least on the business side of the theater business? It seemed crazy, but I wouldn't know until I understood what it was really like behind the curtain. I needed a crash course in the theater business if I was going to consider a career transition in that direction.

This was my opportunity, and I wasn't going to waste it. I had read half a dozen books. I had flown 3,450 miles. I had conducted so many Google searches on the word "assassins" that I was surely on some FBI watch list somewhere, Philly Cheesesteak Kitchen be damned. I certainly wasn't going to let some overly enthusiastic classic rock lovers ruin my big chance. I got up off my Airbnb mattress, banged a broom on the floor like I was in an old-timey cartoon, popped two melatonin, and got back into bed, desperate for sleep to wash over me. I had a big day ahead—a date with destiny, or at least with Darren, the assistant director of *Flying Over Sunset*.

·········

Bleary-eyed, I rolled out of bed at the godforsaken hour of 6:30 a.m., wired and awake. The sun was shining, I was alone, and *Flying Over Sunset* had already been in tech for a few days.

A few hours later, fourth coffee of the day in hand, I walked down Sixty-fifth Street to the Vivian Beaumont Theater at Lincoln Center. My host came to greet me: Darren, the assistant director for the show, with whom I had been exchanging emails over the past week. He was younger than I thought, certainly younger than me, with a slim frame, tight jeans, and sandy hair. He shook my hand warmly and welcomed me into the nerve center of an about-to-open Broadway show.

Technical rehearsals (or "tech," as people in the biz and down with the lingo, like me, call it) happen during a brief window of time between when rehearsals finish and previews—when a show opens to an audience—start. During this very short period, a production moves onto the stage of its permanent home. For weeks or months before this, the cast and creative team of a show will have prepared every element of their performance in rehearsal rooms and back offices. Once they are able to move onto their actual stage, they usually have only two weeks (sometimes less) to translate all of that effort into a fully functioning show with lights, set transitions, and an orchestra, which gets involved only at that very late date.

Tech is the first time a production pulls everything together. All the minutiae—every shift of a prop, lighting cue, costume change, wig fix, and word and step of every actor—are solidified during this period. Then much of it is changed the next day, and the next and the next, even through previews, until the show gets "locked" for the press to review. It is a mammoth amount of work to get done in a tiny period of time for any show, but for a brand-new show like *Flying Over Sunset*, it was positively insane.

The set itself was complex. Towering curved walls that connected to form an open cylinder, sixty feet in diameter, moved around the stage to become what was needed in different scenes: a staircase, a jungle hideaway, a lush California garden. Onto each wall were projected digital images by Beowulf Boritt, a highly in-demand designer who loved to experiment with theater and technology. The end result was going to be incredible, Darren assured me—once it all started to work. In the meantime, the walls had yet to be rigged and automated, so a large team of stagehands was required to move each one as a scene progressed. It took about ten minutes to move one wall.

And that was just the set design. Once the walls were in place, the projections needed to be set, lighting tested, music cues determined, actors positioned on the stage, lines run and rerun and edited and cut. Once everything seemed more or less correct—a process that could take hours for just one scene—they would move on to the next one. The entire show needed to be "teched" all the way through multiple times before a dress rehearsal.

Darren walked me into the theater itself, which was a hive of activity. Although the 1,080 seats were empty of audience members, the room was full with about a dozen large tables, one for each team in the production, littered with symbols of hard work and late nights: laptops, chargers, empty coffee mugs, and extra-large soda cups. There were cables everywhere. "Don't trip," Darren cautioned on our way up, just as I nearly did.

Everyone looked very busy and important, but they smiled and said hello as Darren walked me up the steps and across to row L, orchestra right.

James Lapine, the director, was sitting across the way in orchestra center, deep in conversation with the choreographer. He looked up, spotted me, and waved.

I tried very hard not to die.

Darren sat me behind the table that belonged to the props team. In front of me a young woman with blond hair and glasses too big for her face (the appropriate size to be cool) was Googling desk chairs needed for the scene where Cary Grant and his psychiatrist—who doubled as his father— would deep-dive into his childhood and also tap-dance.

A fake bougainvillea, highball glasses, a plastic sword, a severed head, and other props were heaped on the floor and on all the seats around us. The team had already sourced and selected most of what they needed, but now that the production had moved from the rehearsal space into the theater, many items needed to be reevaluated. A shiny silver tray, for example, which looked beautiful up close, could reflect light back into an unsuspecting audience member's eye. Every single prop needed to be tested and, if it wasn't suitable, replaced. Hence the never-ending online shopping.

Yes! It was early on, but I had already found a job in the theater I was actually qualified to do.

The tech rehearsal started. Then stopped. Then started again. Then stopped. Tech was painstakingly slow. Cues and movements that had been rehearsed for weeks had to change if they didn't work on the much larger stage with the full sets in place. Everything had to be tweaked until it was perfect, and perfection couldn't be rushed.

I came in during a scene where the lead actress playing Clare Boothe Luce is high on LSD, singing the titular song, "Flying Over Sunset," barefoot in her garden. Although it wasn't overly complicated, with just two actors onstage mostly singing and walking, it took four hours to get through it. By the end I knew the entire song—each key change, each pause, each crescendo—so well I could have sung it myself.

Once that scene was "teched," I watched her male counterpart perform a number with the lyrics "I am a giant penis rocket ship," also high on LSD.

Every song was surreal—that was the point of the show—but just sitting in the audience during a rehearsal was an out-of-body experience. Each of the actors turned it off and on in the flutter of an eye. One minute they were normal people wearing T-shirts that said inane things like "There's No Place I'd Rather Be Than Beaver Valley," joking around with their coworkers and sipping iced tea; the next they had transformed into their characters even without the help of costumes, wigs, or makeup. For anyone who has ever worked on a Broadway show, this was totally routine, I realized. But to me, the lifelong fan, seeing how the cast moved through the transition seamlessly, deep in the flow of a song or scene and then immediately stopping for direction, was incredible. They listened or asked a question, a normal human for a few seconds, before jumping right back in where they left off, becoming another person without skipping a beat.

Eight hours flew by quickly in a series of tiny sequences, snippets of songs, and interminable lighting shifts, and I couldn't quite believe when I heard James say we were done for the day. As I packed up my bag to go, he came over to say hello and I dropped my bag at his feet, startled by being so near to the director, *the* James Lapine, writer of *Into the Woods*, Pulitzer Prize winner, regular Sondheim collaborator, who, up close, was just a normal guy with glasses and a plaid button-down shirt.

"Sorry," I said bashfully. "That was so amazing." I could not stop gushing, even though I had not understood the whole thing. "How do you think it's going?"

"There's still a lot to do," he said, reiterating what I had heard from Darren as well. "But we'll get there. What about you? What brings you here to us?"

I gave him the *Reader's Digest* version of my internship journey—looking for a new career, midlife crisis—while simultaneously thinking, "*Oh my god*, I'm talking to a Broadway legend," and trying desperately hard to think of adjectives besides "amazing" and of something intelligent to say about the show besides "I liked the part with the drugs," which was all that was coming to my head at the moment.

"You know, *Flying Over Sunset* is kind of about the same thing," he told me. "People who have been successful in life but who are stuck and need to figure out what to do next."

I had not thought about it that way, but it did resonate. I was stuck, and I was trying to find out what came next. Maybe all I needed was a dose of LSD and a penis rocket ship to get there.

Chapter 3
The "I Want" Song

I have never been a punctual person. For a long time, I blamed this on my Cuban heritage and Miami upbringing, but responding to egregious tardiness with a shrug and a pithy "Cuban time, sorry!" didn't seem to cut it in the professional world, especially anywhere outside of Miami, where that reference meant nothing.

On my very first day of rehearsals for *Assassins*, despite being unable to sleep in my new New York home due to the cocktail of nerves, excitement, and the incessant, blasting bass from the bar downstairs, I got up extra-early. Tardiness is a terrible quality for anyone, especially an intern on a bright, winter Tuesday morning when there would be absolutely no good excuse to show up late.

Unlike in the rest of the world, Monday is the theater industry's "weekend," because most shows perform Tuesday through Saturday. Actual theater professionals spend their Mondays doing extra rehearsals, working out, auditioning for other shows, or taking meetings with their agents. But as a lowly not-yet-intern, I'd had a day as clear of obligations as the sky was of clouds—for the first time in I couldn't remember how long. I took the subway uptown to treat myself to an afternoon at MoMA, whizzing past the crowds staring at *Starry Night* to linger in front of Picasso's *Les Demoiselles d'Avignon* for almost an hour, listening to tour guide after tour guide give their sometimes conflicting interpretations.

Newly installed hand sanitizers hung outside every bathroom, but that was the only indication that anything in the outside world was amiss. That evening I had dinner at a friend's apartment. Outside their building, I ran into their nanny, Rosa, whom I knew very well. I went in for a customary hug, as we Latin Americans tend to do, but Rosa just bowed. "It's this virus," she said to me in Spanish. "I think we should say hello like the Japanese." I bowed back to her and headed upstairs, chuckling to myself at the absurdity of worrying about this thing that was clearly all going to be over before it started. Still, I sanitized my hands after touching the buttons on the elevator.

My first morning on the job, I allowed myself one blissful sip of coffee sitting on a park bench, eavesdropping on the men next to me talking about something that someone had just read in *The New Yorker* that they couldn't quite remember but were sure was very good. Then, coffee in hand, I descended into the depths of the New York subway system, attempted to ignore the faint stench of human urine as I bought myself a MetroCard, pushed my way through the turnstile at West Fourth Street, and boarded a train uptown to the rehearsal venue.

That's right. I boarded a train, which would not be a big deal to any rational New Yorker but for me was a formidable challenge. I had a deep and abiding hatred for the subway. I don't ever get claustrophobic, except when I'm underground with my head buried deep inside someone else's armpit. The whole reason I had rented my extremely loud Airbnb from hell was that it was right next to the Classic Stage Company theater, on East Thirteenth Street. I could walk to "work"— like ten feet.

Little did I know that rehearsing in the actual performance space was reserved for the final few weeks or days before opening. Theaters need to maximize ticket sales, so the time between shows, when a stage lays fallow, has to be kept to a bare minimum. As I found out from the call sheet for *Assassins* that had landed in my inbox the night before, we were meeting that Tuesday at the Manhattan Movement and Arts Center near Lincoln Center, a good forty-four blocks north.

The rest of the call sheet was a mystery. There was a brief, formal note from someone named Carmen—"Hi, attached is the schedule for tomorrow." The schedule was as follows:

10:00 a.m.: AEA meeting and contracts
11:00 a.m.: Meet and Greet
11:30 a.m.: Music rehearsal begins

A few breaks were also noted, as well as the end of rehearsal day at 4:00 p.m.

And that was it. What time was I supposed to show up? I didn't want to crash a private meeting or actors-only event. Then again, I didn't want to be late. A quick Google search showed that AEA stood for Actors' Equity Association, so I aimed for the meet and greet at eleven, which seemed like the most logical place for an unpaid sort-of intern to both meet and greet.

The Manhattan Movement and Arts Center, more often abbreviated as MMAC, was a studio and rehearsal space located on Sixtieth Street on the far west side. In addition to providing a home away from home for many a Broadway and off-Broadway production while it auditions or rehearses, it is also the permanent base of the Manhattan Youth Ballet. The subsequent weeks would include a lot of stepping over and around young ballerinas practicing their splits while crying desperately into the arms of a parent after being cut from a performance, eating lunch, or just generally contorting their bodies into inhuman shapes and making me feel simultaneously old and young again, as it reminded me of the opening scene of the 2000 classic film *Center Stage* (a movie I saw three times on opening weekend).

Even though I had done everything right that morning— left early, mapped myself to my destination, gotten only one coffee instead of my usual two—I was still running late for the meet and greet. Never an expert at the subway, I was particularly terrible at figuring out the difference between an express and a local train. I stood frozen on the platform, wide-eyed as an F train and D train passed me by. Finally, I boarded the B—but my hesitation had cost me precious time.

A few minutes later, I was rising up from underground at Columbus Circle, obsessively checking the time. There were only eight minutes left to walk the several long avenues to the MMAC, so I picked up the pace, hoofing it west on Sixtieth Street, with the Hudson River on the horizon. It was a beautiful day, sunny and clear but unable to decide between spring or winter. My outfit—a thick blue-and-gray leopard-print sweater, jeans, and boots with heels, chosen the night before to balance "approachable" with "professional"—fell firmly on the wrong side of that day's seasonal selection. The warmth of the sun, combined with my nervousness in general and fear of being late, meant I was, naturally, sweating.

Finally, I had arrived. I looked down at my phone again—11:02, winning!—to double-check which room we were in. As I was trying desperately to blot my forehead to look less like the literal hot mess that I was and more like the calm, cool, and collected intern I hoped to be, I did not even notice as I literally crashed into someone walking in right in front of me. "Whoops, I'm so sorry," I said, placing a hand on the shoulder of my victim.

I looked up and only then noticed a very perplexed and shaken elderly gentleman. It took less than two long, horrible seconds before I recognized him as Stephen Sondheim.

He had a shock of white hair and a full beard that still contained flecks of black. In photos, he is always pictured with a wry and kind smile, but mostly he just looked confused as to what had just happened. Our eyes met for only a second as I backed away like a frightened deer. My mouth was attempting to form more apologetic words, but my brain was unable to cooperate. It was composing some sort of Sondheim-esque melody, perhaps—the lyrics were just "Stephen Sondheim, Stephen Sondheim, holy crap is that really Stephen Sondheim?" I think I managed a squeak. He looked away and continued walking in with his companions, who held the door open for him as I sat down to catch my breath.

Day one, and I almost killed Stephen Sondheim. The man was about to turn ninety. It's a miracle that he came away unscathed.

I waited a few beats, watching him enter the building, peering through the glass as the faces of everyone inside broke into smiles. Putting two and two together (*Assassins* was his show, after all), I realized we were probably going to the same place. I didn't want to look like a stalker, so in spite of my tardiness, I loitered outside for a minute or two before heading into rehearsal room 2.

A cacophony of happy voices, the kind people use when they are genuinely delighted to be there, gusted through the open doors. I took a deep breath—no turning back now—and walked in. There were maybe fifty people inside, but the room was huge with high ceilings, so it didn't feel crowded. The director—and my new boss—John Doyle, was standing right next to the door with a radiant smile on his face. I had looked up his picture no less than a dozen times before even leaving London. But to my surprise, he looked over at me and walked straight in my direction. Smiling!

I don't know how he knew who I was—he definitely would not have Googled me, and had he tried, he might have found only my wedding announcement from *The New York Times* in which I looked *way* younger, and less sweaty, than I did now—but perhaps the expression of terror on my face gave me away.

"You must be Alisha!" he said and grinned. "It's so nice to meet you. Is it still okay to hug?" he asked, the term "social distancing" still weeks away from entering common parlance.

"Absolutely," I said.

John was in his sixties, wearing what I came to think of fondly as his uniform: small round glasses, slacks, and a button-down shirt underneath a gray or blue sweater. He spoke with a light Scottish brogue that had been watered down slightly after years of living in America. "Welcome, welcome," he said. "Go mingle. Everyone's here."

The rehearsal room looked like a high school gym, complete with a basketball hoop at regulation height above the wall of mirrors at the back. There were red, white, and blue boxes piled up in the corners farthest from the door. Along the wall to the right of the entrance were a few folding tables covered with a random assortment of props. Although John was known as a minimalist for his deconstructed production style, some things were needed: an empty Kentucky Fried Chicken bucket, a stuffed-animal dog, a fake joint (at least I think it was fake), and a whole lot of guns.

I surveyed the room, assiduously avoiding Sondheim, who was being fawned over by two of the more "senior" cast members (the rest seemed, like me, in awe and terrified to go near him). John Weidman—Laura's father and the writer of the show—was there, chatting with Judy Kuhn, a legendary vocalist whom I had seen in a production of *Fiddler on the Roof* in London a few months earlier that had caused me to ugly-cry all through intermission.

Assorted cast members stood by the mirrors, catching up in small groups about what they had been working on or their second jobs or spouses, including the two tall, handsome leading men. As I eavesdropped, I couldn't believe they were having such mundane discussions. Were these beautiful, supremely talented creatures really just people like me? I was, frankly, too nervous to find out, and didn't dare to go up and meet, or even greet, any of the actors. I spotted a couple of people who looked like they worked in an office—my kinfolk!—and beelined toward them.

The small talk continued for a couple of minutes, and then John Doyle called for attention from the podium at the head of the room. Everyone stopped chatting and the cast took their spots on chairs that had been set up in a horseshoe shape around the piano, with music stands positioned in front of them. The rest of us, mostly staff from the Classic Stage Company's office, stood behind, poised to hear John Doyle, Stephen Sondheim, and John Weidman—three of the greatest minds in American theater—tell us about this richly dark and complex show that would undoubtedly shine a new light on the most critical issues of our time: patriotism, socioeconomic injustice, immigration, and what it truly means to be an American in this day and age.

There was plenty to absorb. The show was based on the historical assassination attempts on nine U.S. presidents, from the perspective of the assassins and would-be assassins themselves. Famous names that are footnotes (or more) in history books—John Wilkes Booth, Leon Czolgosz, Sara Jane Moore, Lee Harvey Oswald—share, in speech and song, their motivation, their hunger for notoriety or fame, and their mental and emotional instability over an intermissionless hour and forty-five minutes.

The musical has been mounted in New York more than once since it premiered in 1990, often at times of great upheaval in American history—during the Iraq war, after 9/11, and now, in 2020. In his original review, *New York Times* critic Frank Rich called it "daring" but also "disorienting," saying it was as if "someone had removed a huge boulder from the picturesque landscape of American history to expose to light all the mutant creatures that had been hiding in the dankness underneath." John Doyle's addition to the *Assassins* canon would be to create a show that was both timeless and a reflection of its current time.

Yes, there were a lot of intelligent things that these three greats had to say about putting on *Assassins* in the era of Trump. There was a photographer from *Playbill* there that day, so there is a record of me, for all of time, at this exact moment. You can just about spot me in the back row, arms crossed in front of me, notebook in hand with my head tilted slightly to the right, looking on attentively. What it did not capture was what was going through my head at that exact moment: Holy shit, I'm actually in a room with Stephen Sondheim.

At some point I was woken from my reverie by the sound of applause—I had missed the entire speech. A stern-faced older woman with glasses was telling everyone who wasn't cast or production that they needed to leave. As they trickled out, I wasn't sure if I was cast or production—or neither?

"Is it okay for me to stay?" I asked John Doyle, still not quite sure what I was supposed to be doing.

"Of course!" he said. "That's why you're here. Take a seat."

The podium had been cleared and in its place were two folding tables and chairs facing the "stage," which for the purposes of rehearsal was a tape outline. It was shaped like a *T* and, in the actual production, would be painted in the colors of the American flag.

The first table I came to had two seats and was covered with binders and folders. The woman who had cleared the room was sitting in one chair, staring intently at her laptop screen. Her glasses were perched low on her nose and whatever she was reading seemed to annoy her. The other chair was empty, so I went to sit down in it.

Without looking up, the woman said, "Not here."

"Yikes, okay, sorry!" I exclaimed, bouncing back up. "Hi. I'm Alisha," I said with a smile.

She didn't look up, uttering just one word: "Carmen."

"Oh, of course, you emailed me. It's so nice to meet you. I'm so excited to be here, thank you so much for having me. Is there anything I can do to help? And where's the best place to sit so I can be out of your way? I'm happy to go get coffee or snacks, just anything you might—"

Carmen looked at me like I had insulted her mother, so I stopped babbling like an idiot and waited for instructions.

"You can sit over there," she said, gesturing to a seat at the other table next to a young woman. "With Molly."

"Great, thank you so much." I was determined to make her like me. "Let me know about that coffee!"

"I don't drink coffee," I heard her mutter as I slunk away.

Carmen was the production stage manager, later described to me as the nucleus of the show. John Doyle had a vision and Carmen made it happen. She was the fixer, tasked with keeping everything together—the actors and their various call times, when they had to be fitted for costumes, whether John wanted the sunglasses in this scene, or if he was getting rid of them. Carmen maintained all the changes and requests with clarity and sanity during the lead-up to the show. Once it opened, she'd be backstage every night making sure everything ran smoothly. She was efficient and smart but terrifying.

Molly, John's assistant, had her nose buried in a music binder, reviewing the notes of the opening song. Her hair was shaved close to her head, her glasses were tidy and round, and her expression was serious. Molly, I would learn, was serious about everything. She brought as much care and attention to the dramaturgy guide, a research document she had compiled for the cast that detailed the history of each character and a summary of the features of each gun, as she did to how the pencils were arranged on our table (in a cup, points facing down).

I introduced myself and made a joke about "dying to be here" which I thought was hilarious but did not even elicit a chuckle. Had I overdone it with the perfume that morning? Or worse, the opposite? There was no time to be offended. The music director, Greg, had sat down at the piano and started pounding a few notes. "Let's start with the first number," he said, as the cast all turned to the right page of sheet music in their librettos. "Three, two, one…"

Long after this day passed, I'm still not quite sure how best to describe it. Among the cast of sixteen were some of the most talented performers on or off Broadway: Tony nominees, TV stars, and one legitimate Disney princess (Judy, who sang the voice of Pocahontas). Even though most of them had not yet memorized the music (unlike me, who had replayed it on Spotify over and over again before touching down in New York), they still sang clearly and (mostly) correctly from the notes. You'd think that in the weeks I sat in the rehearsal room listening to the same few songs over and over again, I would eventually get bored, desperate to check my phone. I did not. They were incredible and sang for what seemed like minutes but was more like hours, stopped only by Greg or John periodically to correct a note or try something in a different octave.

When break was called (at the regular interval determined by Actors' Equity guidelines), I snapped out of my trance. Although it was the first day, no one had taken me up on my offers of assistance. Carmen and Molly, when they did deign to look over at me, were only giving me side-eye. I needed to win them over so they would give me actual tasks to do. I was determined to not just observe but actually work, even if that work only entailed serving coffee. (Or tea? Maybe Carmen liked tea?)

Break wasn't long, but I rushed back to Columbus Circle and up the escalators of the Time Warner Center to Bouchon Bakery to pick up a secret weapon: two bags of Bouchons, delectable, bite-sized, melt-in-your-mouth, moist brownies. Baked goods, like puppies and rainbows, could only inspire love. They had never once failed me in my quest to make friends.

I walked back and delivered the bags straight to Carmen's table, looking at her expectantly, like a kitten who had caught a mouse. "Would you like a brownie?" I asked with what I hoped was a smile that could melt her icy heart.

"No," she deadpanned.

I was crestfallen. "Oh, do you not like chocolate?" I said, making a mental note of her preferences so I could do better next time.

"I love brownies," she replied. "But I've given up sugar for Lent. It's killing me just looking at them."

The second half of rehearsal was as mesmerizing and, for me, as unsuccessful as the first. After one particularly stellar song, I turned to Molly. "Would it be weird if I clapped?" I asked.

"Yes," she responded, rolling her eyes.

When rehearsal finished, everyone started packing up their things to go. "Can I help clean—like sweep or do anything at all?" I asked Carmen and her assistant Derek.

"No," they said.

"All right then, I guess I'll see you all tomorrow!" I walked out of the MMAC into the fresh air, with my ego a little bruised but my belly full (someone had to eat all those Bouchons) and my soul fuller, even more determined that tomorrow I would find something useful to do. I checked my phone. It was full of messages from my husband, my parents, and my friends: *How was it? What did you do? Did anyone throw coffee in your face yet?*

I didn't know what to say. How do you respond when you've literally had the chance to live out your childhood fantasy? I was elated, naturally. The high that I normally felt after seeing an incredible show was not too far off from that of the protagonists of *Flying Over Sunset*. Everything seemed brighter and fresher than it had when I had walked in that morning and inadvertently almost knocked down a legend.

If I squinted, it was like I was *in* a musical. I was just about to jump on the nearest lamppost and spin around it while bursting into song. Except that a car sped through the yellow light at the corner of Sixty-first and Amsterdam, nearly hitting a biker, who banged the hood and started yelling obscenities while people honked in the background.

Back in reality, I considered my situation. I had to make friends. Most reactions to my presence that day had ranged from apathy to loathing. I had to actually learn what was happening around me. If this fantasy could transition to a real-life career—and that was still, just one day in, a major *if*—then there was no time for dancing in the rain. I had a job to do.

The opening number of *Assassins*, which I had heard no less than a dozen times that day, features a refrain. Like all important parts of a musical that the writers *really* want to make sure you remember, it gets repeated again and again throughout the show. Upbeat and cheery, the Proprietor sings about happiness as the ultimate goal. Through verse, we're told to not stay mad because life's not that bad. That everybody has a right to be happy—and that everybody has a right to their dreams.

In this particular show, the sentiment is extremely ironic. It's sung to, and then by, a gaggle of criminals who believe that the one thing standing in the way of each of their dreams is a sitting U.S. president that they need to kill. But I wasn't thinking about them. I was thinking about me.

How long had it been since I had been happy? For so long I thought the pursuit of happiness had been what was guiding me, but now I wasn't so sure.

Back in the fall of 2005, I was living in New York, as were most of the people I knew. Like a flock of migratory birds who had doused themselves in the ubiquitous gender-neutral fragrance CK One, my college classmates and I descended on the Big Apple after graduation, determined to make our mark on the big city. I had my entry-level consulting gig at the now defunct business-and-strategy firm Monitor Group. I knew nothing at all about business or strategy, but the people who interviewed me thought I was likable and smart enough to do the job well. Hiring me was, in retrospect, a terrible idea on their part, but I was so relieved. I had a job offer. I had a boyfriend (Carlos!). I was old enough to drink and had enough income to pay first and last months' rent for a tiny studio in the East Village.

It should have been the perfect time in my life. Except it wasn't, starting with a tour of the Monitor office, a completely nondescript Midtown high-rise. The first stop was the nap pods on the eighth floor. "That's awesome," I whispered to one of my new coworkers. "You can just nap during the day if you really need it."

"Not exactly," he whispered back. "It's for when you finish work at 2:00 a.m. and have to be back in the office by 5:00 a.m. and don't have time to go home and sleep. They'll even send out your clothes to be dry-cleaned overnight so you can have them back by the morning."

A few weeks later, after midnight, I was walking down the hallway when I heard a sound like muffled tears. Through the crack of the door, I overheard one of the firm's few female partners on the phone. She was softly weeping as she explained to whomever she was conversing with that after returning from her (very short) maternity leave, she found out a person she previously hired had been promoted above her. "And I haven't seen my baby in three days," she wailed.

I knew then that I had made a terrible mistake.

Monitor was a work-hard, work-harder culture, and as junior consultants at the bottom rung of the corporate ladder, we were expected to be on call all the time. That demonic red blinking light of my BlackBerry, signaling I had a waiting email, haunted me day and night, even at Sunday brunch. I had dreams where I threw it into the East River and never looked back. I had nightmares where my fingers grew too big to press the buttons and I couldn't turn it off no matter how hard I tried.

There was a tiny voice in my head telling me I should try to find something else, but it was drowned out by the louder voice of my father: Leaving before at least two years was stupid. Work wasn't supposed to be fun, otherwise you'd be paying your boss, not the other way around, and don't forget the signing bonus you had already spent and then some.

"Stay the course," Dad advised on the phone. "With two years in that job under your belt, you'll be set up to do anything else you want."

The days were long and punishing. My main client was in New Jersey, which meant I had to wake up at five each morning to be in their offices by eight and often wouldn't get home until well after ten at night. Plus, the work I was doing—helping to create a fast-track marketing plan for a drug that cost twenty thousand dollars a year if someone was lucky enough to have insurance—felt pointless and hollow. I had spent the better part of the last five years studying gender and all the awful injustices in the world that people faced. Every morning when I looked in the mirror, wearing a boxy, ill-fitting suit that was not designed for someone with boobs but did make me feel like a kid trying to dress up like my dad, I felt I was doing nothing—absolutely nothing—to make anything in the world better for anyone at all.

Then, a few months into the job, on a nippy December Friday when that festive feeling was hovering in the air, I went to blow off some steam the only way a twenty-three-year-old knew how: happy hour. I ended up at B Bar in the East Village, known then for its open courtyard and irresistible two-for-one deal on drinks.

It was one of those glorious nights where the cocktails and chat were ample and generous, the friendships random and unexpected. I bumped into Jess, a friend from college, who was sipping a half-price mai tai. I hadn't seen her since graduation, about a year and a half ago, and she updated me on her love life and work life and her roommates' lives too.

I asked her what she was doing for work. "Corporate philanthropy consulting," she said, something I had no idea was a real job you could get paid for.

She explained a little more about what she did with as much coherence as she could manage and I could absorb (see: two-for-one drinks) as Ja Rule's scratchy growl blasted over the speakers and some people created a makeshift dance floor in the middle of the patio. We exhausted our conversation and made a move to join them.

She gave me her number and said to call anytime. "Email me your résumé too, I'll pass it along." With a flurry of air kisses and promises of getting drinks soon, she was gone, not realizing she had set me on a course that continued for fifteen years.

In a matter of weeks, that random encounter turned into a job offer from her company. Working there was everything I thought I'd ever wanted. It was a job with purpose, better hours, nice people. But it required a pay cut, paying back the full amount of my already-spent signing bonus, and an irresponsible-looking four-month blip on my résumé.

When I went home for Christmas to my parents' house, I was still in a quandary about whether to stay at Monitor or leave. Nathalie, my best friend from childhood, and I were at the beach (Miami is glorious in the winter, our most smug time of year) snacking on Doritos and Oreos (gotta keep that beach bod) while I churned through my options (indulge me, I was twenty-three). There were many downsides to leaving, but if I had a chance to follow my passion, work with friends, and find more joy in my every day, shouldn't I?

"Are you happy?" Nathalie asked, looking at me over her sunglasses. "If you're not happy, you should leave. If you're happy, you should stay."

This was, of course, a question that privileged twenty-somethings have the luxury of asking. Even then I realized how rare it was to consider happiness a factor in my decision-making. My parents, whatever they thought about my schemes, had always provided me with a critical safety net—a debt-free college education and a standing offer to pick me up and dust me off if and when I inevitably fell. Without them, there would have been no decision to make. But I did have a choice. They were willing to help me pay back my signing bonus if I sent them fifty dollars a month for the next ten years. I quit Monitor the first Monday of the new year.

I vowed then and there never again to make professional decisions just because they were easy or convenient, to always chase work that would truly make me happy. But now, decades later, back in New York once again and only a few days into my musical theater internship, I realized it had been a long time since I had asked myself that question. When was the last time I had really checked in with myself to see if I was, indeed, still following my heart? I couldn't honestly remember. And I wondered if I hadn't asked it before because I had been afraid of what the answer might be.

Assassins rehearsal complete, I headed back in the direction of Lincoln Center, passing through the stage door like an old pro this time, ready to sit in on another evening of *Flying*

Over Sunset tech. Darren, the assistant director, came to get me and filled me in on what I had missed: not much. A whole day had passed, but they had moved forward at a snail's pace and were still on act 1.

One of the leads, Harry Hadden-Paton, who played Aldous Huxley, was sitting in a chair alone onstage as different parts of his face were projected on giant screens behind him. The resolution faded in and out until someone shouted out their approval, at which point he was asked to move, almost imperceptibly—a turn of the head, a pout of the lip—and the process was repeated. This went on for well over an hour; long enough for the woman at the props table in front of me to have ordered no less than six different types of fake vines and some sort of treatment to make the top of a desk sticky enough so Tony Yazbeck, who played Cary Grant, would not slip off when he tap-danced on top of it.

I took the opportunity to eavesdrop on the production team, who were arguing about adjusting the mic placement on the lead actress's wig—it was giving her headaches, apparently, which set off a list of to-dos that involved the audio team, hair and makeup, costumes, and the choreographer. The show was like a living organism, and each department, while master of its own domain, had to operate fluidly and collaboratively. A small script change might result in a need for a new prop, or modification to a lighting cue, which impacted the direction and, ultimately, what the actors did. They had to cooperate and everyone had to do their part, or the whole thing would fall apart.

Although everyone was supremely professional, tensions were high. Most shows that open on Broadway are mounted out of town for audiences a few times to test songs, messaging, and general reaction before people invest the colossal amount of time—and money—that it takes to bring a show to Broadway. Once a production arrives in New York, there is usually some sense of how a show will do based on the result of those shows, called tryouts. Not only is this useful knowledge for the artistic team, but it's also vital insurance for investors, who, in most cases, are required to put up all the money for a show well before it opens.

Flying Over Sunset had been in development for more than four years and gone through a series of workshops (a simple, bare-bones production of a show that is used to work out kinks or attract investors—or both), but few people outside of the tight-knit New York theater scene had seen the show. There was definite anxiety about how it was going to be received; a new musical not based on a movie or the back catalog of a pop artist was always risky anyway, even if it had the opportunity to delight spectators from Connecticut to California before making its way to the discerning audiences of the forty-one Broadway theaters in New York City.

Tech wrapped a few hours later, which gave me time to score a half-price ticket to the gender-swapped *Company*, which was in previews on Broadway after its successful London run. Humming the theme song and feeling very much like Bobbie herself, I walked downtown on foot and made my way to the theater as the sun went down and the lights of Times Square illuminated the sky.

That night, in a taxi home, I felt like I could finally respond to my barrage of texts from earlier. I sent one to my husband, fast asleep in London, that read: *Today was amazing. If this was it, and I had to come home tomorrow, it would have all been worth it.*

Chapter 4
The Eleven O'Clock Number

I was spending my days in rehearsals for one musical, my evenings in tech for another. Who cared that the world was more or less imploding around me and I hadn't gotten a good night's sleep in days? I was on Broadway, baby. Now what I needed was to actually do some work. Rehearsals for *Assassins* seemed to be going swimmingly, but besides grinning like an idiot every time they finished a number or scene, I had done nothing for the first few days. I tried, probably too enthusiastically, to offer assistance to anyone who needed it. *Can I throw away that apple core for you? Would you like a snack?* Everyone politely demurred. These actors. They didn't know the first thing about having an intern. Where was my *Devil Wears Prada* experience? Why hadn't anyone asked me to pick up their dry-cleaning or yelled at me because their soy latte was actually made with almond milk?

Frustrated and useless, I took matters into my own hands. I started refilling the water jug at breaks, unasked. To the untrained eye, this may have seemed simple, but it was perilous. I had to step over at least two to three supine ballerinas just to reach the water fountain. Then I had to monitor the water level in the jug and fill it up before being asked. It required a lot of attention and a weird fixation with how much people were hydrating, but I was never one to shy away from hard work.

Over the next few days, I found more ways to help. I used the skills I had perfected as a cheerleader for more than a decade to make very encouraging faces at the cast when they performed: smiling, winking, nodding intensely. I tried to replicate the experience of a live audience, but they may have thought I was having some sort of manic episode.

My initiative paid off. After a few days of asking—begging—to please do anything else, Derek, Carmen's assistant, took me up on my offer and asked me to help prepare the room for the next day when rehearsal was done. After the actors and musicians left, I gleefully picked up trash, humming whatever tune had been practiced that day, folded up the chairs, and set up music stands for the following day's rehearsal.

I called my dad on the way home to tell him about all my new responsibilities. He let out a laugh. "So . . . you left your job, husband, and kids to clean up after other people?" he asked.

Normally a snide comment like that from my father would have given me pause, but that day, it didn't faze me. Like so many children of immigrant parents, I realized from an early age that the investments made by my parents and grandparents were all meant to pay dividends with my generation's success. No one ever said this to me outright—*You are the manifestation of all our hopes and dreams for a better life so don't screw it up and also please pass the chicharrones*—but I always knew it was true.

Every family story told about the past conveyed this in subtle or not-so-subtle ways. I once asked my dad why he preferred Whoppers to the (clearly superior) Big Macs. He explained that, in middle school, he would spend hours both before and after school folding and distributing newspapers on a paper route. His salary went to my grandfather, to support the family's needs, but his tips were all his. He diligently saved some but each week would take thirty-seven cents and go to Burger King. There, using both of his newsprint-covered hands, he ate a Whopper, relishing each bite.

Now here I was, ladies and gentlemen, the embodiment of the American Dream. I was the one who never let people down. The responsible babysitter, the straight-A student, the Harvard grad, the good girl. And now, the cleanup crew.

I couldn't have cared less; I loved my new responsibilities. As far as I was concerned, I was moving up the ladder quickly and was well on my way to becoming indispensable. And anyway, I figured he was just jealous. I knew he would have given anything to be in that rehearsal room alongside me and gladly pick up any amount of trash for a chance to go behind the scenes at a musical.

As I settled in to my job, I was better able to observe the different roles around me. It was a lot to take in. Putting on a show anywhere already requires a multitude of parts, and not just the ones onstage: set design, costumes, directing, producing, music, acting, choreography, and so on. But in New York, the complexity was astounding. The sheer number of unions that needed to be contracted with (the Broadway League alone negotiates with fourteen) was enough to make your head spin.

The nuances of the whole machine were discouraging. This was no minor career shift. Let's say I wanted to produce—why not? I had great contacts going for me, but so did a lot of people. Even Molly, whose dad was a leading Broadway producer, was struggling to get jobs and to produce her own work. Theater didn't seem like a meritocracy at all—you could be good, really good, either onstage or off—but there were so many people that were really, really good who were unemployed.

On the production side, Derek told me that he estimated probably 90 percent of his fellow stage manager union members were not working at any given time. He had trained as a Pilates teacher (a much more stable income than theater) and fit that in during his spare hours (ha!—like there were any between job hunting, rehearsing for one show during the day, and managing another in the evening) to ensure he could pay rent. And this was someone who was successful, working regularly, and making a living in the business.

I couldn't see where I could fit in beyond making lots of money doing something else and then investing in shows as a producer, which was also a risky proposition. Industry averages estimate that only one in five shows makes back its initial capital. "Pretend it's money you'll never see again" is what insiders say. That didn't suit my current financial situation either.

Though the path to a real job ahead was murky, I was genuinely just so happy to be sitting in that room, observing, listening, learning, and filling up water jugs. Just the feeling of being part of a production was enough of a new and wonderful experience.

Unfortunately, outside of the blissful cocoon of rehearsals, the situation was less upbeat. It was literally downbeat. As in, I could still hear every downbeat of every song played by the bar downstairs throughout my entire apartment. Trying to solve the problem, I ventured into the bar around 1:00 a.m.

It was completely empty, save for one lone bartender crooning along to Fleetwood Mac (ironically, of course). He was a stoned twentysomething with four-day-old stubble and, ugh, a beanie, who intentionally ignored me as I wandered in.

I smiled and introduced myself, then I politely asked if he wouldn't mind turning down the music just a smidge—on account of there not being a single customer there. He just looked at me wild-eyed, like I was some middle-aged Medusa, and proceeded to turn the music up louder. I stormed out, furious, but the music stayed at that ear-splitting volume until four.

I was very, very tired. In my life, I was no stranger to sleep deprivation—the first few months when my twins came home from the hospital, everyone had said "sleep when the baby sleeps," but no one had told me that two babies would not necessarily sleep at the same time—but that didn't make my current situation any less exhausting.

And then there was this virus. It had been newly christened COVID-19, and things were getting increasingly apocalyptic over in Europe. On our calls, Carlos assured me that he still wasn't panicking, but he was slowly buying up bags of pasta and rice (so . . . panicking). Several countries had begun issuing orders restricting movement.

In New York, however, things still felt more or less normal. The most visible change was the addition of hand sanitizer as the new "must have" accessory. People were Purell-ing nonstop. I got into a cab and the taxi driver asked if I wanted some; he pulled out a five-liter jug of it. "Walmart, yo," he told me when I inquired where he had found it. "On sale."

I was anxious and edgy. Lack of sleep plus pandemic panic equaled low levels of emotional resilience. I walked down Fifth Avenue and burst into tears at the sight of an advertisement with a French bulldog wearing a party hat, which reminded me of my precious pooch back home. What I really needed was a hug—but no one wanted to risk the germs.

After rehearsal, I was live-chatting about the noise situation with Airbnb back at the apartment, still sniffling, when a text came through from Laura, who had moved to New York after finishing her year of travel and was working in the city for a big nonprofit.

My favorite intern! she said. *Want to meet me for dinner?*

I was waffling. I was so tired and my bottom half was already in sweats. In the fridge was leftover Chinese take-out from the night before. The Airbnb chatbot and I were becoming friends—*I'm so sorry*, chatbot said to me, *everyone deserves a good night of sleep*—but my complaints about the noise were leading nowhere.

Screw it—I threw on some jeans and hopped in a cab. When I got out, Laura met me at the corner and pulled me into a giant embrace. Everything finally felt like it was going to be all right.

We ate a mountain of dumplings and then followed a text from her friend to a launch party for a shoe store, for a free beer and a crowd of people at least a decade younger than us. The evening was rejuvenating. What was I moping around for? I did not need my once-in-a-lifetime opportunity to be ruined by a stoned bartender with mainstream taste in music. A few clicks of my mouse and one angry letter to Airbnb later (*It's not me, it's you*), I had slammed the door shut on "the noisiest apartment in New York"™, left the plants to fend for themselves, packed my bags, and moved into the Ace Hotel.

Once I got there, everything fell into place. My room was heaven. It was trendy, industrial in decor—all exposed pipes and concrete walls—and much smaller than my Airbnb but equipped with everything I needed: a minifridge, a bathtub, and a record player with a dozen records from Prince to Arcade Fire. Downstairs there was a coffee shop and a Milk Bar, which sold eight different types of cake. My first night, I took a slice of rainbow birthday cake up with me to bed. I was Eloise, resplendent, well rested, and unashamed.

········

From then on, I settled into a comfortable routine. I set my alarm for 8:00 a.m., threw a sweater over my pajamas, and headed down to the lobby with my laptop. After some friendly banter with the baristas, I balanced my cappuccino in one hand and my computer in the other as I found my spot: the tall table with the high stools just next to the bar.

For the next forty-five minutes, I begrudgingly allowed my "real job" my attention. I hadn't told many clients what I was doing, saying only that I would be on New York time for a few weeks. It didn't seem worthwhile to spook anyone, especially when I was planning to return in just a few weeks. Or so I had told most of them.

The business day in the UK was already in full swing by then, and I worked as efficiently as possible. Sign here; review a memo there; respond to clients; and delegate, delegate, delegate. Nothing was challenging, but it all felt tedious. I counted down the unread emails—twenty, fourteen, four—that stood between me and Broadway.

Somehow, I felt deceitful. My digital self, the one attached to my work email address, was plowing along like nothing had changed. But inside it felt like everything had. I didn't miss the work, or my clients, or taking hour-long meetings or editing strategy presentations. I was making promises and setting meeting dates for April, when I'd be back from New York, but I could not imagine actually going to them. The here and now, the rehearsal room—that was the place I wanted to be. Forever.

By 10:00 a.m., I was back at the MMAC, sitting on my folding chair next to Molly, who blocked me from Carmen's view. I waltzed in, squirting sanitizer on my hands and saying hello to the desk attendant. I had been making a concerted effort to arrive ten minutes early so I could fill up the water jug and the tea kettle and do one last sweep of the room to clear any garbage that had been missed on my cleanup the night before.

"Morning," I chirped at Katrina, Whit, and Brad, three members of the ensemble who were tuning their instruments in a corner.

"Hey, hey, hey," I said to Greg, who was reviewing the score for the songs we were working on that day.

"Hi, Carmen! How was your night?"

Carmen looked up at me over her glasses. "Fine," she said. It was an improvement over the previous day's "hmmph." I'd take it.

After the water was replenished and niceties dispatched, Carmen got up to close the door at exactly 10:00 a.m. and called out that rehearsal had begun. Strict timekeeping was an Actors' Equity requirement. Rehearsal start and finish times were set, called, and recorded in a book. Actors were entitled to breaks of fifteen minutes within any three-hour working period and an hour for lunch. Part of the production team's job was keeping an eye on the clock.

As a director, John was famous for his stripped-back productions—minimal sets and props—which allowed the actors to go deep into their roles and really shine. He talked about Brecht a lot. My notebook was covered with starred and circled notes to myself: *Look up Brecht. Who the hell is Brecht?*

(Brecht: A German playwright who developed "epic theater," the art of *Verfremdungseffekt*, which aims to alienate or distance the audience from what is happening onstage. For bonus points, try to say *Verfremdungseffekt* three times fast.)

Many of John's shows featured actor-musicians, a role he both invented and cultivated. Actor-musicians both play characters and play instruments onstage. In interviews, John speaks about the origin of it being from a place of necessity—a limited budget meant limited cast size, which meant that having actors who could double as the orchestra was as efficient as you could get—but it's now become an artistic choice for productions far beyond his control or vision.

Katrina, Whit, and Brad were some of the actor-musicians on *Assassins*. They were extraordinary. They each had to sing, act, dance, move through the stage and the audience, and play at least two musical instruments per song: acoustic or electric guitar, oboe, clarinet, flute, mandolin, violin, viola, banjo, harmonica, accordion, and a few strange items whose names I did not know. The whole cast was supremely talented, but actor-musicians' work had a "tapping your head while rubbing your belly" quality to it. They were gifted multitaskers (and not just because, I assumed, they had to belong to not one but two unions).

That morning, the actor-musicians were learning the choreography and movement for "How I Saved Roosevelt." The song volleys between a perky, upbeat, brass-led bop, sung by the actor-musicians, who play witnesses to the attempted assassination of FDR, and a haunting solo by the assassin in question, Giuseppe Zangara. The number juxtaposes members of the crowd, who are telling news cameras what they saw, with Zangara strapped to an electric chair, about to be executed for his crimes.

Zangara was played by Wesley Taylor, an actor who had recently portrayed Plankton in the *SpongeBob SquarePants* musical on Broadway. He was not an imposing figure before rehearsal—thin and not much taller than me, dressed in the ubiquitous Roots-branded sweatpants—but once the first notes came on, he was transformed. He belted his part each time with such urgency and pain that it was hard to believe that just moments before he was laughing while sipping a green juice. As more or less the only audience member, he would lock eyes with me every time he sang, each time sending shivers down my spine.

Between Wesley's lamentations, the actor-musicians were on fire. Not literally, but actually if John had asked, they probably would have agreed. They were up for anything, which was good, since that was more or less what was required. Over the course of four minutes and fifty-two seconds, they had to, in rapid succession, or often at the same time, do the following: move boxes onto and around the stage; add sunglasses to their costumes; sing; play their instruments; switch instruments (sometimes having to climb a ladder to get the new one); play the new instrument; and avoid obstacles while marching up and down, onto and off the boxes they'd previously carried onto the stage, like the world's most sadistic step class. And then the number would be over, and they'd get ready to rehearse it all again, until lunch.

John would stop, sometimes midphrase, to fix a note or make a change. His method was Socratic by nature, questioning the cast on their opinion about the characters and their motivations and then gently guiding them in the direction he wanted. No matter how absurd the request ("Let's try it this time walking backward, while playing the clarinet, in heels"), they did it. Often John would suggest something I thought was crazy, until it was performed—then it was clear why everyone called him a genius behind his back and sometimes to his face.

At break, I asked around for coffee orders now that people had finally started to give them to me. List in hand, I rushed out to Birch Coffee, a few blocks away.

Break time in New York often coincided with dinnertime at home in London, so I FaceTimed Carlos's phone. Lola's face greeted me on the other end.

"Hey, Mommy," she said, with a small pout to her lips and a downcast expression.

"Hey, babe! How was your day?"

"Fine," she said sniffling.

"It doesn't sound fine." I stopped at the corner of Columbus to wait for the light to change. "What happened?"

"Mia and I got into a fight. And she said she didn't want to be my friend anymore." At this last statement, her voice broke.

The light turned green so I crossed the street, telling her how sorry I was, explaining that all friends fight and that I was sure they would make up tomorrow. By the time I was standing outside Birch, she had calmed down.

I was just about to ask her to put Theo on when she said, quietly, "Mommy, I miss you so much. Why aren't you here?"

Guilt crashed through my chest. Here I was, gallivanting around New York City, living in a hotel, surviving mostly on coffee and cake, and having, frankly, the time of my life, while my daughter really needed me. So did Carlos, although he was loath to admit it. That morning, we had argued about the kids' screen time. We both knew our fight had nothing to do with screen time, of course, and everything to do with the virus. While I was still making jokes about how my hands had never before been this clean, it was undeniable that things were rapidly shifting. Among my unread emails that day were one from my doctor back in London (*Wash your hands through two verses of Happy Birthday!*) and one from my bank (*Stop panicking amidst this market volatility, everything is going to be fine!*).

Carlos was understandably stressed: alone with the kids, watching the news obsessively and panic buying. ("I'm not panic buying. I just don't see why having extra dried shiitake mushrooms is a bad idea," said the man who had never cooked with a dried mushroom in his life.) In the middle of our screen-time fight, he suddenly went quiet and said, "You're not here." His voice was cold. His breathing was ragged and audible. "You don't get to be a 'backseat parent.' You don't have a say." I started to yell that there was no such thing as a backseat parent, that you were always a parent no matter what side of the ocean you were on, when he hung up on me.

With Lola, I was even more confused about what to say and resorted to my worn-out mantra: "I know it's hard, but I'm so grateful that you guys have let me come to New York to have this amazing opportunity."

A message from Molly flashed across my phone, asking for a triple-shot Americano and reminding me that rehearsal was starting up again in ten minutes.

"I have to go, okay?" I told my daughter. "I love you. I'll call you back later and we'll figure out this Mia thing."

As I ordered the coffees on my list, I tried to put my conversation with Lola out of my mind, but I felt like such a terrible, selfish mother. My twins, still my babies at just eight, were too little to be left without me for so long. Carlos was lashing out because he was freaking out, whether he was prepared to admit it or not. The likelihood that we were living through the first few chapters of *The Andromeda Strain* was increasing by the moment. And I was at a Midtown Manhattan coffee shop, balancing drinks with both hands and waiting for someone to come hold the door for me so I could make it back to rehearsal before Carmen locked me out due to Equity rules. What was I doing?

And then I remembered the last ten years.

·······

In eighth grade, when I eventually learned where babies came from (late, having been given a fairly accurate representation by a friend at age nine and assuming it was so unbelievably gross that she must be lying), the whole thing seemed remarkably straightforward: lots of sperm vying for the attention of a very small egg and one gets lucky; then, nine months, one gender-reveal cake, and at least two baby showers later, a baby comes out. Ideally, while one is heavily medicated. Simple.

Carlos and I got married young, the same age as my mom and dad—twenty-five—which isn't empirically that young but these days seems like it was a shotgun wedding with me the child bride. Right from the start, we knew we wanted to have kids together, but there was no great urgency. That was, until an ovarian cyst showed up ("It's the size of a golf ball!" my gynecologist told me with an unnerving level of enthusiasm), leaving me with just one working ovary.

All of a sudden, a horrible thought appeared that had never before existed: What if I can't have kids? My biological clock, to which I had never paid much attention, was sounding an alarm. Carlos agreed. We had to get started right away.

As it turned out, my own experience with the birds and the bees wasn't nearly as straightforward as my health class textbooks made it seem. Instead, it was arduous and terrifying and included miscarriage, loss, and the unexpected news that both my husband and I carried a recessive gene that could affect my ability to carry a healthy baby to term.

Eventually we ended up in the office of a fertility clinic that smelled like lavender and promised that with science, test tubes, and a whole lot of money we probably should have been saving for retirement or using to buy a house, we, too, could have a baby—a healthy baby. Some of this was crazy (pulling one cell out of an eight-celled organism to test its genes), some scary (700 million blood tests and daily self-administered shots in my abdomen). I feel to this day unbelievably lucky to live in a day and age where technology could help make that happen.

After many injections and suppositories and all manner of indignities in public bathrooms around London, we harvested my eggs, combined them with Carlos's swimmers in a petri dish, did some fancy science stuff, and came back with two embryos ready for implantation (with five "on ice" for the next round, if we wanted). And then I held on for dear life.

Luckily for us, so did those sticky little embryos, because a few weeks later we went in for a scan and were told there was not one but two heartbeats thumping around in there. There was surprise and tears of joy. And Carlos's immediate insistence that, if they were a boy and a girl, we name them Luke and Leia. All of which was quickly supplanted by my gynecologist's lecture on risk that played on a loop in my head. There were so many opportunities for a twin pregnancy to go wrong, and after so much had gone wrong already, I was morbidly convinced that it would.

So I ignored my swelling belly and people asking if I was gaining weight. We told almost no one that I was pregnant, even as I passed twenty weeks and was very obviously pregnant. "Are you still seeing that personal trainer?" my coworker Rosanna asked, flicking her eyes down to my bulging belly as

I heaped a second scoop of french fries onto my plate in our office canteen.

"No, I should really call him again, though," I replied with my mouth full, unable to resist shoving a few fries into my mouth before paying.

Eventually we did tell people. Everyone was so excited, talking about miracles and rainbow babies, but frankly I was having none of it because I was in complete denial that I was even pregnant. I'd get excited when they arrived, I told myself. And not a moment before.

The pregnancy was stressful and excruciating. I had weekly scans to check the health of both babies, and, when one was smaller than the other, they told me to prepare to deliver as early as twenty-four weeks if there was an emergency. I stuck my fingers in my ears. I eschewed a baby shower and bought only the bare minimum: two car seats and one crib (babies are tiny, and they can share). I'd get excited when they arrived.

Miraculously, after almost three months of drinking four protein shakes a day and taking two very painful nurse-administered steroid shots in the derriere, I gave birth to two supremely tiny but adorable and healthy babies five and a half weeks before their due date. They needed two weeks in the hospital to grow and develop their suck reflexes, but then, on Thanksgiving, two years after my first miscarriage, we bundled them up in a taxi and brought them home.

As a result of having ignored my entire pregnancy, my first reaction when I stepped through the threshold of my house with a kid in each hand was "oh shit." I was completely unprepared to be a mother. And that was before the sleep deprivation kicked in.

I'd tell you about the first few months, but I can't, because I have completely blocked them from my mind. They are

gone. I know there was a short-lived attempt at breastfeeding; a lot of late-night calls to my aunt, a pediatrician, asking
well-meaning but for the most part very stupid questions; and
something called tummy time. Videos exist of this period of
my life, which have replaced the blank space in my head where
my memories should be, but I don't remember anything that
wasn't captured on a screen. I was tired all the time. I never
got to the point of seeking help for depression, but I cried a
lot. In fact, I probably cried more in the first two years than
the twins did, and that was saying something.

When the twins were about four months old, I decided to
brave leaving the house for a playgroup I found on Facebook
for twin moms. I was terrified to take them out on my own a
lot of the time in the early months, because I didn't know how
I would physically handle both of them crying at the same
time without my assortment of pillows and play mats and
diaper genies, but I needed adult company and I thought other
twin moms might understand my unique predicament. When
I got to the community center, both of my babies were mercifully sleeping, although the room was cacophonous with the
voices of many toddlers, running around the room in pairs.

A woman walked up to me with a cup of tea. "How old are
they?" she asked.

"Four months," I said.

"How's it going?"

I gave her my well-rehearsed response, the one people wanted
to hear: "Oh, it's fine. Hard, you know. But so worth it."

She took a sip of her tea. "Really? Because until my twins
turned one, I felt like I was living in a war zone. It was horrible."

I looked at her, and promptly burst into tears. "*I feel that
way too,*" I practically screamed. "I'm so glad you said that."

She patted me on the shoulder. "I promise, it gets better."

She was right. It did get better. And better, and better. They got older and more fun. I started to feel more like myself again and not just a sack of milk or an encyclopedia of nursery rhymes. But they still required a lot of care—at least until this year, this wonderful year when they had their own friends and social lives and didn't need, or even want, my undivided attention.

For almost a decade, I had been focused on getting pregnant, being pregnant, and then taking care of babies, toddlers, kids. It had taken me years to truly understand how much I had given up—and gained. Even my professional decisions had been made to pursue not just what I wanted but what we, as a family unit, needed: income, stability, and flexibility.

Now, however, I had two moderately self-sufficient eight-year-olds. And thanks to Carlos I had a few weeks to contemplate my needs, my wants, and to consider what else I had been missing. As I slid into the rehearsal room just before the break ended, as much as I knew I loved my daughter and understood she missed me, I also knew I had a responsibility—no, an obligation—to make the most of this break from my life that I had been given.

....

The song "Unworthy of Your Love" is *Assassins*' only attempt at a classic romantic duet, but it's among the weirder scenes of a show filled with weird scenes (like when one character does a cakewalk dance en route to his own hanging). That afternoon we were rehearsing a scene and song with just two cast members: Tavi Gevinson, who played Lynette "Squeaky" Fromme, and Adam Chanler-Berat, who played John Hinckley. Both Fromme and Hinckley are creepily obsessed with celebrities—Charles Manson and Jodie Foster, respectively—and sing, together but each addressing the object of their fixation, about how they want to prove themselves worthy.

Throughout the course of the song, and their spoken scene preceding it, Adam and Tavi had to find the absolute depths of obsession to deliver something believable and, ideally, even a bit relatable for these supremely unlikable would-be assassins. Tavi, belting at the very top of her range (and even attempting beyond it) would throw herself on the floor, belly down, beating her fists on the ground; Adam tried out a nervous tic and sat in a corner hugging his knees to his chest.

Onstage, in costume, in front of an audience and under the spotlight, this commitment to their craft would win them raves, but here in the rehearsal room, I just felt embarrassed for them. This is, of course, what actors do. Or the good ones, at least. They put themselves out there, they don't care what they look like or sound like, especially when they are rehearsing. They commit and give 1,000 percent. And that was the piece of it that I thought, at the time, was embarrassing. Because that sort of display of authentic emotion—in public!—terrified me.

As a kid, I wasn't this way at all. I loved to sing. At age five, I got up in front of my entire elementary school and belted out "I Gotta Crow" from *Peter Pan* in the talent show. The moment was captured on video and I still cry now when I watch it. People were talking in the background—you could even hear some kids laughing—as I really got into the crowing part in my homemade green tie-dye outfit and jaunty hat. But I was glowing. I was singing my heart out and it didn't matter what anyone else thought.

But then puberty hit and I reacted by becoming extremely self-conscious about performing. When I switched schools in eighth grade, it wasn't at all cool to be in chorus; I was so determined to fit in that I buried my passion for musical theater. Until, that is, the summer after my freshman year. I had scrimped and saved from my two part-time jobs to afford a plane ticket and a two-hundred-dollar registration fee for a volunteer position at a summer camp in an ex–coal mining town in the north of England, halfway between Newcastle and Durham. I flew over the ocean and landed in London after a sleepless night. One hour-long Tube ride and a three-hour train later, I was met on the platform by a few of the local volunteers from the community center where the camp took place. With its traditional high street that included the chippy (fish-and-chips shop), a pub, an off-license, and a working men's club, Stanley looked much like every other northern English town, but I didn't know that at the time; to me it was thrilling and new.

The trip was memorable for a lot of reasons. I bonded immediately with the other volunteers, some from just down the street and others from abroad like me, over hard work and the idealism that comes with being young and having the good fortune to travel. We worked together, made breakfast together, and slept on mats on the gym floor together each night.

But the main reason I'll always think fondly of Stanley was the karaoke night at the pub. We had plied ourselves with enough beer to make getting up and performing "Sweet Caroline" to a room full of out-of-work miners seem like a great idea.

Even though it had been years since I had sung in front of anyone, when the book finally came my way, I chose a belter: "Crazy" by Patsy Cline. In short order, the DJ called my name, so I pounded a shot of Goldschläger and marched up on that stage. I took the mic, closed my eyes, and sang with my whole entire heart.

I have no memory of the song, except that I know I didn't hit all the notes, but when I finished, the applause was deafening. "You're an amazing singer," my new friends said. Even the miners offered to buy me a round; one had tears in his eyes.

Their praise, heaped on that night and throughout the following weeks, gave me the confidence to audition for an a cappella group back at Harvard. I got in, which was a huge boost to my ego. For two wonderful years, I sang and performed regularly. I really loved the applause, but truthfully I always got nervous before being onstage and struggled to overcome that feeling of self-consciousness, the worry about what other people thought. Whether I was good enough. I was always holding something back, keeping a piece of my heart just to myself.

Once I graduated, I sang from time to time (usually when there was alcohol involved) but never thought about really committing to it and never dreamed of pursuing it professionally. I made safe choices, the ones that didn't cause me to fear my heart would get trampled on if I left it all out on the stage.

I thought about what I had given up to keep on the smart, steady, practical path as I watched Tavi try the scene again, this time with more writhing. That's why I was here. To get uncomfortable, to retrace the steps of the course I didn't take. To ask myself the hardest question: What had I lost, or missed, by giving up on pursuing a creative outlet in a serious way?

"The point of theater," John had said during rehearsal, "is to remind us of who we are." In that room, it seemed like there was a small possibility of that happening to me. And though I couldn't put that into words that my eight-year-old daughter would understand, it was the real reason that, in spite of everything happening around us, I couldn't go home yet.

Chapter 5
The Finale

For most of the final forty-eight hours of my internship, I didn't realize it was the end. I was still so sure that everything was going to work out, that people were overreacting, that this whole virus business was going to blow over and we'd all be laughing about it for months to come.

"Lockdown" had not yet crept into my vocabulary, but despite my blind insistence that nothing was changing, things had started to feel different. News about the virus was getting worse by the day, and cases in New York were increasing. It was a Wednesday morning and I called Rebecca, my friend from our London girls' weekend, to see if she had time for coffee later—I had a two-hour break that evening between *Assassins* rehearsal and the *Flying Over Sunset* dress rehearsal, the final run-through before previews began the following day.

"You won't believe this," she said, "but we're in isolation." The parent of a student at her son's school had tested positive, so the entire school was sent home as a precaution. "We're not supposed to leave the house for fourteen days," she said.

Someone was screaming for an iPad in the background.

I sent my love, made a mental note to send some Milk Bar cake too, and boarded the subway uptown. It was strange: the car was emptier than usual and a handful of people were wearing masks. I didn't have one but wrapped my scarf around my mouth just to be polite. Anytime someone coughed, the entire train stared daggers at them. I had to blow my nose but resisted until I was on my own.

I arrived at the MMAC a few minutes early, squirted some sanitizer on my hands, hopscotched around the stretching ballerinas, and got to rehearsal room 2. The desk where Molly and I had sat had been removed, so I threw my stuff on the floor next to where she was already sitting, stewing in discontent.

"What's this all about?" I asked her. We were almost friends at this point; I had been warming her up slowly, using my women's studies credentials to cement my reputation as a legitimate feminist and casually dropping a Judith Butler reference into a conversation while wearing a "My Body, My Space" T-shirt.

"They said it was for more room, but why our desk?" she said, adjusting her glasses. "Ugh, the patriarchy. Let's grab a drink this week and we'll chat about it more."

"For sure," I said and nodded. Personally, I didn't mind sitting on the floor but didn't want to damage our budding solidarity.

I started on my morning tasks: filling up the water jug and the tea kettle, arranging the music stands for the first song, making sure everyone had pencils and their scripts. Before rehearsal kicked off, we had a virus briefing from Toni, the executive director of Classic Stage Company, who oversaw the business side of the production. She had come to reassure the cast about the measures the company was taking. "We're doing everything we can," she said, detailing how they were disinfecting the theater, requiring the cast to enter and exit only from the stage door, and banning backstage guests.

Everyone nodded along with her speech, but their faces showed a range of emotions. Some were worried already and had heard about show cancellations and whole casts being struck down with the virus through Broadway back channels. Others were unbothered or, like me, in denial. This was, after all, the industry whose motto was "the show must go on."

"What are you going to do?" Bianca, one of the actor-musicians whispered in my ear while Toni was going on about cleaning procedures. "Do you have to go home?"

"I'm here until theaters close or borders do," I told her, repeating out loud what I had been saying to myself for days.

Toni wrapped up her talk and we started rehearsal. The plan was to run through the first half, which up until that point had been rehearsed only scene by scene. It was relatively smooth, particularly considering that John's organic style meant that the cast had to be constantly adjusting and adapting. ("Do it in a Russian accent! Hats on! Hats off! Put the box stage right, keep the box stage left!") The cast responded willingly with enthusiasm, as Carmen took down every note. Even sans costumes, lights, and staging, you could begin to see how things would come together for the audience.

At lunch, Carmen asked me to buy her an orange and said thank you to me when I handed it to her. I may have even seen a hint of a smile. During the afternoon slot, I spent about an hour with Derek, helping him tape pockets into the prop purse that Sara Jane Moore (would-be killer of Gerald Ford) would carry. "We need one to fit the gun, one to fit the lipstick, and a third for a dead dog," he instructed.

I diligently measured the pockets for size, overjoyed to have a real task that would be part of the performance.

("See," I would tell my dad later, as I sent him a still from the show. "See that purse? *I taped those pockets myself!*") After rehearsal, I cleaned the floors, organized the music stands and chairs, switched off the lights, and left the room for what I did not know would be the last time.

I had a few hours to kill before *Flying Over Sunset*'s dress rehearsal, so I went to grab a quick bowl of ramen at the Momofuku in the Time Warner Center. I sat at the bar, slurping my noodles as I watched the headlines scroll across the screen: Borders sealed in Ireland. Schools in France were closed. The line graph of cases was starting to trend upward. It was like a scene from *Contagion*. I called Carlos, scared and frustrated in equal measure. He and the twins were still booked to fly to New York in three days, and as far as I was concerned, that wasn't changing. He was having second thoughts.

"I think things are going to get worse," he said. "What if we get stuck in the U.S.?"

"This is going to blow over," I said, my voice ratcheting up to a higher frequency. "As usual, the newspapers are making a bigger deal of it than it is. Case numbers are still small. Plus, they can't just close the border. At least not without a few weeks' notice."

I spoke with more confidence than I felt, because deep down, somewhere, I knew he was right. Every minute had begun to feel like borrowed time, with a doomsday clock counting down to, well, doomsday—but I just didn't feel like I was ready to leave this little fantasy I had made for myself just yet.

We hung up without a resolution and agreed to talk in the morning. I left half a bowl of ramen uneaten and walked over to the Vivian Beaumont Theater. I was milling around in the lobby with a handful of others waiting to be let into the dress rehearsal when my phone buzzed with a text from my mom, telling me that an usher at one of the Broadway theaters had tested positive for the virus. My parents were scheduled to fly into New York for the weekend too, but they couldn't decide if it was still a wise idea.

Things were moving so rapidly, and everyone was uncertain as to what was coming next. The crowd at the dress rehearsal that night had been invited by the cast, creative team, and crew, so many knew each other, but you could see the awkward pauses when people came to greet their friends. Do we hug? Shake hands? Fist-bump? There was nervous laughter all around, poorly masking the fear underneath each greeting.

We were asked to leave empty rows between groups. A woman near me had disinfectant wipes in her hand and was cleaning her seat before sitting down. It felt eerie and surreal, but at seven thirty, when James Lapine took the stage with a microphone, I swallowed all those thoughts and pushed them down deep.

"I'm not sure if you've ever been to one of these before, but this is the point where the director comes out and lowers your expectations," he said to chuckles—some more nervous than others. "I hope you have a great 'trip.'"

When I had left my final tech a few days before, it seemed to me like there was still a lot to be done. Truthfully, I wasn't sure if they were going to be able to pull it off. Had the cast figured out the timing of the percussive dance steps? Did they coat the table with some sticky substance so Tony could tap-dance on it without falling? Had the props girl found the perfect fake plant (of the three thousand I had watched her buy) to adorn the garden scene? I had been privy to all of the small details and hiccups. Part of me wondered whether this would impact how I experienced a show. Watching a great musical for me had always been like having an out-of-body experience. I become completely immersed in the performance, transfixed, until the lights go up again. What if that magic was gone now that I had watched the process?

I needn't have been concerned. As soon as the very first note was played, I was captivated. It turned out that it didn't matter one iota that the last time I saw the lead actress sing her teary, emotional number, she was wearing a onesie. When she came onstage in full costume, it felt like the first time. It was magical for me in the way only musicals, especially those of Broadway caliber, can be.

The first half seemed to go off without a hitch. Most of the kinks had been worked out and no one in the audience would have been any the wiser about the amount of time spent in the previous weeks debating just where Henry's mic should be placed in relation to his hairline.

By the time intermission rolled around, I couldn't believe how quickly the first act had passed. It was nine o'clock, and I did what all well-bred theatergoing ladies did at intermission: raced like a crazed maniac down to the bathroom, bracing myself for the interminable line. With only a hundred people in the audience, though, I breezed right in for the first and probably only time in my life. I washed my hands for twenty seconds, joking about it with the lady washing next to me.

Walking back to my seat, I turned on my phone. I had thirty-eight messages. The United States had announced it was banning all incoming European flights. Borders were closing. It was time to go home.

I was overwhelmed with emotion. And fear. And to-dos. My brain wanted to launch into immediate planning mode (rebook flight; cancel hotel reservation; figure out how to get to the airport; stock up on coffee beans), but for once in my life, I shut it down, the way actors did stepping onto the stage, tuning out regular life to focus only on the lines and play in front of them. I had come this far. And though I hadn't yet figured out if I was ever going to be a Broadway singer (probably not) or find some way to translate my online shopping skills to become a props master back in London (not sure) or sign up for community theater or just remember this as the dreamiest two and a half weeks of my life, there was no way on earth I was going to miss the second act. I couldn't risk not knowing the ending of the show. It was the one bit I hadn't seen in tech and that was still evolving; the music team, Michael Korie and Tom Kitt, had still been rewriting the final song that very morning.

I shot off a quick reply text to my parents, who were responsible for at least seven of the thirty-eight messages I had received. As the lights went down, I asked them to get me on any flight back to London for the next night and said I'd call them back after the show. I turned off my phone again and put it, and all my anxiety, away in my purse.

The second act was . . . trippy. Literally. The entire final piece took place while the leads were on acid. There were swirling colors, a gigantic palm frond (nicely done, props team), and one scene where people were possibly drowning. But the audience was into it. When the giant penis rocket ship song came on, the whole audience guffawed, myself included. Maybe they had a hit on their hands.

When the lights went up and the applause died down at about 10:45, I found Darren and James and thanked them both profusely.

"Will we see you at previews tomorrow?" Darren asked.

"They're closing the borders," I said, my voice wavering as I tried very hard not to cry. "I have to go back to London." After a congrats, I walked out of the theater, pausing briefly by the stage door that I had walked through for the first time just a few brief weeks earlier. The time that had passed between then and now wasn't empirically long, yet it felt completely life-changing already. I knew a little bit about being behind the scenes on Broadway (I could define "sitzprobe" and also, finally, quote Brecht), but mostly I realized how little I actually knew. And now it was over. Was it really all over? Just like that?

Back at the hotel, there was so much to do, and I just didn't feel prepared to process what was actually happening. There were flights to cancel, calls to make, regrets to silence. Before heading back to my room to start what would become months of my own insane-sounding Google searches that were straight out of a dystopian novel ("Yeast next day delivery," "Best face masks for kids," "How to decontaminate groceries"), I made a detour to the Milk Bar in the lobby. If there was ever a time for a gigantic piece of five-layer rainbow birthday cake, this was it. I finally drifted off into a restless sleep at 2:00 a.m., with only half of my to-do list completed. It would be my last time enjoying a hotel bed for a very long while.

When I woke up the next morning, I was depressed and freaking out. I half-heartedly drank my coffee in the lobby in my pj's and posted to Instagram an image of the words printed in gold at the bottom of my mug: "Good Luck."

Luckily, as far as *Assassins* was concerned, things were business as usual. Toni had finally taken me up on my offer to help out in the office and asked me to come in. I had one more day of internship before the curtain came down.

The rehearsal was closed that morning—John was working one-on-one with Andy Grotelueschen, who was playing Samuel Byck, Nixon's unsuccessful assassin, who had a deeply disturbing monologue to deliver. It would be just the two of them in the room, so with a few hours free, a bit of room in my suitcase, and impending doom everywhere around me, I went to stock up on what I thought I might need to survive a pandemic overseas: two dozen cookies, six pounds of coffee beans, and every box of mac and cheese the 7-Eleven around the corner had in stock.

As I checked out of my room at the Ace, handing over my keys, I cried. "I'll be back," I promised the receptionist. She nodded—the way you do to crazy people—then sanitized her hands.

Walking downtown, I took my time, trying to soak it all in. One of my favorite New York activities has always been eavesdropping on street conversations. In the weeks prior, I had heard a bro in a baseball cap tell his friend that he was going to smoke all the weed in the city that night and listened as two girls, fluidly switching back and forth between English and Spanish, discussed one of them attending her ex's wedding: "I'm so down to go *pero tenemos que ser incognito*, okay?"

That morning, all anyone could talk about was the virus. One young woman, toting a yoga mat on her back, was crying into the phone, telling her sister how worried she was about Grandma. A couple was arguing about how much toilet paper was too much (answer: there is no such thing as too much toilet paper). A well-dressed woman pushing a dog in a baby carriage was telling a friend through her AirPods that she heard you could catch it from mosquito bites.

The severity of the mood on the street contrasted completely with what I found when I arrived at the Classic Stage Company offices. The sentiment inside was light and breezy with the young, energetic staff gossiping about weekend plans and recent victories in the spring sales. No one seemed to be bothered by the pandemic panic outside.

I greeted the team, many of whom I had met in the previous weeks, and found Toni. Everything from fundraising and
marketing to budgeting and managing suppliers fell under her
purview. She walked me over to a cubicle in the corner. Most
of the desk space was taken up by giant stacks of paper: hundreds of invoices, receipts, deposit slips, contracts, and bank
statements were lined up precariously, needing to be sorted by
date, alphabetized, and filed.

"We had an office assistant doing this for us," she said.
"But she left. Six months ago."

In my normal professional life, it had been years since I
had to file anything for myself and, indeed, years since I had
even seen a file. But in the back end of the theater business,
technology seemed to have stopped in 1999. Even paychecks
were distributed to actors in person as actual checks.

I sat there grinning like an idiot. The world was crashing
around me but I had a pile of dusty, redundant, obsolete paper
to file. It was perfect for my unsettled mental state: work that
requires just enough of your brain that it's hard to dwell on
anything else.

Oddly, it also opened a door in my mind. No, I wasn't
going to be a Broadway star or director, not without a lot
more training, but I did know my way around running a company and there is no better way to learn about a business than
by filing its paperwork. In just a few hours, I had gleaned
more about what was needed to run a small theater than I
had from all the books I had read beforehand. The glamour
of rehearsals was only the tip of an iceberg filled with bills for
waste management, exterminators, agents, rehearsal spaces,
and sometimes even custom-made candy for each production.

As much as I learned from attacking that stack of paper,
what was most evident was that there was so much I didn't

know. This was a whole different side to the industry—that I had the chance to glimpse only through invoices and contracts—and an important one, especially for me. If I had been able to stay for a few more weeks, I would have picked up so much more. COVID was forcing me out of New York and away from a deeper understanding of what it would really take to run a theater.

But as it was, I was left with just the intriguing wisp of an idea: Did I want to run a small theater one day? Or produce? Or be involved with local theater, not as a full-time job but perhaps on the side of some new profession that really was perfect for me? I didn't know—but buried in the filing cabinet was a little (metaphoric, nonflammable) spark of hope for the future.

A few minutes later, Toni came out of her office and asked the staff to huddle up.

"I know you're all worried about this virus stuff," she told the team. "We are monitoring the situation closely. The Broadway theaters are all still open and so are we. If people call about ticket sales, tell them we're still proceeding as normal."

The team nodded and asked a few questions, mostly about logistics—what they should post on social media or say to the box office staff—and then they went back to work. I, too, turned back to my filing stack. Not three minutes had passed when Phil from marketing let out an audible gasp.

"Broadway's gone dark," he said. "They're shutting down all the theaters until at least April twelfth."

Everything went silent. Then several colorful curse words blew through the room. Toni picked up the phone and started making calls. The team didn't quite know what to make of it. Someone wondered aloud if she'd get a refund for the tickets she had for *Hadestown* that weekend. Everyone was in a state of shock. The show that always went on was not going on—for a month at least. Broadway had never, in its entire history, been closed for that long—wars, terrorist attacks, strikes, and even the 1919 Spanish flu pandemic had shut theater doors for only a few weeks max.

It was like watching the beginning of a horror movie, when you know something bad is going to happen to the pretty girl alone in the house, but she doesn't realize it yet. All of a sudden, everyone turned frantic, racing around the room from desk to desk and making hushed phone calls to friends who worked on other shows, so I sidled back to my filing cubicle and continued until I had finished putting every single scrap of paper in its proper place. Once done, I examined the clear desk with pride and sadness. The same thought had been going through my head on a loop since the night before: Was this really it? Was it all over?

I went to Toni's office but her door was closed. Through the window I spied her still on the phone, her brow deeply creased as she rubbed her temples with the free hand not holding the phone. I waved and backed away. She, understandably, couldn't meet my emotional need for a ceremonious goodbye while her entire industry was collapsing around her.

I went back to my filing corner to grab my bags when Brendan, one of the marketing assistants whom I had met at the meet and greet, came over. "Hey, are you busy?" he asked. "There's one more thing we'd love your help on."

I jumped up so fast I nearly crashed into the filing cabinet I had just spent hours meticulously organizing. "Absolutely anything. What is it?"

"The *Assassins* costumes are being delivered tomorrow so we need to clear the dressing room," he said. *Dracula*, the previous show, had just finished its run. "We'd love your help down there if you have the time."

I could have kissed him. Except that involved germs. Instead I hurriedly grabbed my bags and coat, unable to temper my excitement of being able to go backstage in a dressing room before I left New York, maybe for good. Brendan walked me down the seven blocks to the theater. He was remarkably upbeat given the impending doom around us. Stunned, and hopeful that his normalcy would rub off on me, I went along with it. We chatted about his plans for the weekend—he was going out to visit his parents in New Jersey—as we took our time walking through Gramercy Park and down into the bustling East Village.

In a lull in the conversation, something in me snapped. "I just can't believe this is happening," I said. "The last time I remember feeling like this was just after 9/11. I was a sophomore in college. A bunch of my roommates were from New York and after the second tower fell, it was this weird mix of panic and also feeling like we needed someone to tell us how to act. None of the grown-ups knew what to do and it was terrifying. You know what I mean?"

"Not really," he replied. "I was in preschool when 9/11 happened."

Of course he was, I thought as I was jolted back into reality. I was technically old enough to be the mother of this twenty-three-year-old kid, my temporary boss, whom I was looking to for reassurance.

"Don't worry about us; we'll be fine," he said. "We don't open for over a month. Theaters will be open again on April twelfth."

Brendan didn't know then—none of us did— that the shutdown would last for more than eighteen months. Countless jobs were lost in the process, not to mention lives of legends like Terrence McNally. Even after theaters were allowed to reopen in 2021, with masks and vaccines mandated for cast, crew, and audience, the ongoing pandemic caused cancellations, uncertainty, and low ticket sales that shuttered dozens of shows. The aftereffects would last for years to come.

But on that spring day, as Brendan and I wandered down Third Avenue in no particular rush, New York seemed like its normal self. The magnolias were flowering, dropping their pink-white blossoms in a carpet under our feet. Kids were walking home from school with parents or nannies, telling tales of their daily adventures with effusive hand gestures. Taxis honked their horns at Ubers, who honked at pedestrians, who flipped a bird and paid no mind.

At the theater entrance, Brendan buzzed me in and told me to ask for Chelsea. I wished him luck and he laughed, as if he wouldn't need it. Off he went, joining the rest of the people to-ing and fro-ing importantly on the crowded sidewalk.

I entered a narrow hallway flanked by a bulletin board full of Equity messages on one side and cubbies on the other. The paint was fading and the lights were low. I was taken aback—I had expected big, glossy mirrors with bright lightbulbs, silk robes with fur collars, a real Patti LuPone–as–Norma Desmond kind of extravaganza—but soon learned that in theaters where space is at a premium (so, every theater in New York City), you're lucky to get a dressing room at all. This one had just two spaces—one for the women and one for the men—and it would be a tight squeeze when the whole cast was in there at once. *Assassins* didn't have any costume changes—how did everyone manage with a show that did?

My musings were interrupted by the arrival of Chelsea, the dresser. She had short curly black hair, glasses, and a big smile that set off her dimples. "This," she said and gestured at the washing machine, "is the most important thing here." She explained, as she showed me how to cut seams from the laundry bags, each named for the previous cast, that a large portion of her job is doing laundry. "Especially undergarments."

Yes, that's right, Actors' Equity specifies everything from break times to unmentionables: shows are often required to provide undergarments for the cast to wear under their costumes. I also got a chance to explore the new and fascinating world of dance cups, which are basically jock straps for dancers. I certainly did not expect that my last intern task would be folding new pairs of undies and sorting them into size and color boxes, but what can I say, it's the glamour of showbiz.

This was one of Chelsea's first jobs and, she told me, her dream job. She had always loved the theater and fashion and had been apprenticing on *Dracula*. Working on *Assassins* for her was the start of her career, building up her résumé and providing a steady income.

Chelsea left me to my folding and told me I could organize the empty hangers when I finished (which I did, by size and color, a deeply satisfying activity). I was glad that my hands were occupied with a repetitive task, because my brain was all over the place. So was my heart.

Like Brendan, Chelsea did not seem overly concerned by the shutdown and how it would affect her first real costumer role. But I was. My heart ached for her and what was to come, but even my pessimism about the future could not have predicted how long it would go on and how decimated the theaters would be.

I thought about Chelsea a lot in the weeks and months to come. About all of them: John and Judy and Brad and Bianca and everyone whose entire livelihoods had been stopped with, for months on end, no indication when they would restart. And, selfishly, I thought a lot about me. How my own dream had been cut short and possibly had ended. How I had tried as hard as I could to run as far away as possible and, just two weeks later, was about to board a flight back home, back to my life and job and husband and kids, and pretty soon, it would feel like it hadn't even happened at all.

Once I had finished folding my final pair of boxer briefs, Chelsea told me I was "good to go" and thanked me for my help. I didn't hug her, even though I wanted to, but gave her a lame elbow bump and grabbed my things.

As I turned to go, I couldn't resist a peek at the bare stage. The production team had removed all the vestiges of *Dracula*, and the *Assassins* setup wouldn't start until the following day. I stood center stage and closed my eyes, imagining an audience filled with anticipation of the opening chords about to be played. It was a future that seemed like it would never happen now. I took a deep bow to the empty room, savoring my last moments as a theater intern, or maybe as an intern altogether, and then stood up and silently walked out the stage door for the last time.

Chapter 6
Stasis

"Hey."

"Hi," I replied.

Carlos crouched down to meet my gaze. "What are you doing down there?"

"I'm sitting under the table."

"I can see that," he said, in the measured voice you might use to negotiate a hostage crisis talk with an angry toddler. "But why are you sitting under the table?"

"I'm trying to calm down," I said.

Crawling under the dining-room table and sitting there, silently, was a tactic my daughter Lola had recently invented. During home school with Mrs. Mommy, math was our worst session. I got frustrated with her; she got frustrated with me. We yelled at each other and blew up and ended the lesson in tears (both of us). But one day, when she got particularly mad at me for not explaining clearly enough why ¼ + ¼ did not, in fact, equal ⅔, she discovered the world underneath the table. She stayed there for about a minute. Then she came back up, calm.

"Are you okay?" I asked. But she looked okay. In fact, she

looked remarkably more relaxed than she had when she went down there.

"I just breathed really deeply," she said. "And stayed still. Until I felt better."

One thing college taught me: adopt the strategies of clearly intelligent people. Especially when those people are your daughter. I studied the grooves in the hardwood floors and focused intently on the dust in the corner of the table leg that the vacuum never managed to reach.

"Okay . . ." said Carlos, sitting down beside me. "Can I do anything?" he asked.

"No," I said, my eyes red and puffy, my entire being overwhelmed and discouraged.

He held out his hand and helped me up from under the table.

I pulled back my hot-pink exercise headband. "I'm done anyway. I have an eighties one-hit wonders barre class in five minutes."

I positioned myself in front of our wall-mounted forty-nine-inch TV, which now doubled as classroom, Zoom HQ, and, yes, a home gym. I tightened my ponytail. And got ready to join exhausted, terrified, out-of-shape women all over the world in my newly minted position as a fitness intern.

········

The first great lockdown of 2020 will be the sort of thing our grandchildren ask us about. Where were you when the lockdown happened? What did you do? What was your experience during this extraordinary time in human history?

When I was in eleventh grade, I had a similar discussion with my own grandmother, interviewing her about 1965 for a school assignment. That was the year in which she, along with her parents, husband, and their five children, was exiled from Cuba and moved to the United States. In a series of conversations, I listened as my *abuela* spoke about the reasons our family left—the rise of Castro and communism and the restrictions on religion that she, a devout Catholic, could not live with. She recalled with clarity the day when my uncle came home from school and told her that the teacher had said Fidel was more important than Jesus. That was the moment, she told me, when she made the decision that it was time to leave the country she loved.

She told me all about the nuns, friends of hers from childhood, who had helped the whole family escape to Mexico, and tearfully waving goodbye to them on the tarmac in Havana. She told me about waiting in Mexico for what seemed like forever, but was just a few weeks, for their visas to come through. She told me about arriving in the United States in Shreveport, Louisiana. The end. Happily ever after.

When I showed my finished report to my dad, he read it and then put it down, pressing on the bridge of his nose. "Didn't you like it?" I asked.

"Yeah, it's a great story," he said. "It's just not true." And then he told me the version he saw through his own eight-year-old eyes, pieced together by his own memories and conversations with his sisters and brothers over time. Back in Cuba, he said, my grandfather was a farmer who had been drafted by the U.S. CIA to report on Cuban agricultural statistics. A friend of his from childhood, Fidel's own brother (as legend goes), came to the door to tell them my grandfather had been outed as a spy. He was an enemy of the state. If the family didn't leave immediately, he would face imminent arrest.

So they fled. Valuables were sewn into the linings of jackets. Excruciating decisions about what to take and what to sacrifice were made by everyone (my dad's biggest regret was their dog, Campeon, who was left behind). My grandmother's friends, the nuns, did help them get passage to Mexico; that part was accurate. But my grandmother never told me about how, when they arrived, their family had a dwindling supply of money and radio silence from the CIA about when they would be allowed to cross the border and enter the United States.

My dad's most vivid memory from that period of his life was one Sunday at church in Mexico. After the priest had completed his sermon, he told the parishioners about the exiles from Cuba and the current plight of my grandparents and their children and asked the congregation to give generously. This group of strangers dug deep into their pockets to support foreigners, people they had never met; the collection plate that day contained enough to buy the food they needed to keep them going until the United States allowed them entry.

"But why didn't Abuela tell me any of this?" I asked him.

"She doesn't remember it that way," he said.

Even at sixteen, I knew that it wasn't that she was lying to me. The story she told me was true to her, just not to anyone else.

All of this to say that memory is a funny, selective thing. I'm not sure which bits of 2020's first lockdown will stick in my mind in the years and decades to come or what I will tell my future grandchildren. Will I focus on the positives: enforced family time, slowing down enough to watch the seasons change, perfecting the art of the homemade dumpling? Or will I instead share with them the negatives: the constant fear, overwhelming worry, the anxiety we all felt anytime anyone coughed or sneezed? The disastrous time I tried to make sourdough?

There's at least one thing that I know will remain in my mind for years to come in permanent marker: those confusing, terrifying first few hours back in London after my dreams of Broadway had unceremoniously exited stage left.

For most of my seven-hour flight home from New York, I managed to sleep with the help of my good friend melatonin, waking up only as we touched down, greeted by gray, gloomy London skies. The city looked exactly like it had when I had left only two and a half weeks earlier, and maybe that was why it felt so surreal. Surreal to be back so soon, so unexpectedly. Surreal to be texting back and forth with Carlos about essentially fleeing our home in London to travel up to the Isle of Skye that night—typically a sixteen-hour journey but this time with a suitcase full of "essentials" that included the dried mushrooms, the four crazy gas masks, and five kilos of coffee beans.

At the house, Lola rubbed her eyes, maybe thinking she was dreaming. "I thought we were meeting you in New York," she said, as I hugged her on her bed.

"Change of plans, babe," I said, with as much cheer as I could muster. "Mommy's home."

Three years ago, we had bought a place on Skye, one of the remotest parts of Scotland, as a vacation home. Our house wasn't big but was comfortable for a family of four and idyllic, tucked into a quiet wood, bordered by a creek and a lot of sheep. When we first got the keys, we joked that the rural location was perfect in case we were ever invaded by aliens or zombies. Never in our wildest dreams did we actually think we'd need to escape to it for real.

Carlos's relief to see me back in London was nearly palpable. His shoulders were tight and I could tell he had been a ball of tension since the moment I left. "We need to be mentally prepared to be gone for four to six weeks," he whispered, as we went around turning off heaters and outlets, pulling down blinds.

When I look back, I can't believe our optimism. As we packed up to leave our house for what we thought would be a temporary period, my own emotions vacillated between feeling guilty that I had left him to shoulder all of this alone and resentful that I was back at all, instead of in the *Assassins* rehearsal room with a bagel and schmear, following along with my copy of the libretto while eyeing the water jug to ensure it wasn't empty.

Things snowballed quickly. Seven days later, schools were canceled and no one was allowed to leave their homes without an approved excuse. I was frantically buying yeast in kilograms, and we were privately wondering if we needed to withdraw our savings and stash the cash under our mattress in case the entire banking system collapsed. My two brothers, both in San Francisco, were already locked down; my parents in Florida refused to believe anything was really happening. I was in my own bizarre tech rehearsal, but we never made it past the same scene and it seemed pretty unlikely the show was ever going to open.

Although we were extraordinarily lucky, and certainly luckier than most—we were able to work, had fresh air, and never, ever ran out of toilet paper—we were paralyzed by fear. And hostage to time. The days dragged on and on and on. The school hastily set up a Google Classroom filled with assignments the children were meant to complete and PowerPoint presentations we, as parents, were supposed to deliver. While Carlos and I first tried to divide up the tasks evenly, it became clear that my temperament was better suited to the task of "homeschooling." I was bad at it, but he was worse.

Initially, I was a pretty lax teacher, assuming we'd be back in real school after the Easter break, so it wouldn't matter much if the twins completed the worksheets they were assigned. At my real job at I.G., we went into crisis mode—helping people get what they needed so they could work from home and reassuring clients that although things were very unusual indeed, we'd be "business as usual" for their needs. My team, none of whom had children to terrorize with home school, picked up a lot of my slack. In our social lives, we diligently scheduled weekly Zooms where we hosted pub quizzes and drank virtual cocktails with best friends and college roommates, before the novelty of it all wore off. We read the news obsessively, watching the number of deaths tick upward in a sweep of red ink.

Time in lockdown was marked by bags of pasta or flour purchased, chocolate consumed, jars of moisturizer used. About fourteen bars of chocolate in (so, a week), I opened a tube of tomato paste that was set to expire four weeks after opening and wondered to myself if we'd still be stuck in Skye when it went bad. By the time we got to month two (40 million bars of chocolate consumed), my emotions were all over the place.

There were occasional days where I felt, "*Yes*, I can do this, I was built to manage a global disaster scenario, now someone hand me a pencil so I can teach about Queen Elizabeth I with my right hand while dialing in to this conference call with my left."

But most days I fell somewhere on the spectrum between terrified and depressed. I was going stir-crazy, cycling through the seven stages of grief—shock, denial, cookies, brownies, tiramisu, apple crumble, and cinnamon rolls—and trying to be optimistic about the future. Before I left for New York I had secured a second internship, a posting at Christie's auction house in London scheduled for May. I had always loved the art world, and before I got on the corporate philanthropy track, I seriously considered working in galleries or museums. The internship at Christie's had been sold to me as a true internship experience. I'd join a group of real interns (by that I mean young people, just starting out in their careers), helping research and price works in the famed auction house's Post-War and Contemporary Art Division. I had foolishly held on to the idea that everything would be back to normal by late spring, at least in an office, if not on a Broadway stage. But I was wrong. I got the email: the internship was indefinitely postponed.

In the grand scheme of what was going on in the world, it was empirically a small setback. But now that I was confined to the four walls of my house, juggling everything, but this time without the village of helpers and friends, it felt like the nail in the coffin of my dreams. No more internships. No more new adventures. No more exploring future career paths. I was just here, hiding under the table or baking something that required at least four cups of sugar. I was going to be here forever.

Chapter 7
Britney, Whitney, and Me

The first rule of lockdown is "You don't talk about lockdown." Lockdown sucked for everyone. Even if you had it pretty good, as I undoubtedly did, the monotony was endless. Although I had a long list of things to accomplish each day, I was full of ennui. I didn't want to do any of the things I had to do, like laundry and dishes and conference calls and home school and more laundry and more dishes. At night, once the kids went to bed, I would fall on the couch exhausted, even though the longest walk I had done that day was from the twins' bedroom to the office and back. Mentally, physically, emotionally, I was atrophying.

Of course, I had coping mechanisms: wine, sugary treats, and Instagram. I was on the sofa one night, about four weeks into lockdown, with all three (peak lockdown!) and scrolling down the endless photos of children's art projects and nature walks with very depressing captions when I reached a bright spot: literally bright. A young woman, dressed in a matching sports bra and leggings made up of purple, yellow, green, and pink squiggles, hearts, and triangles, was doing jumping jacks to the sound of a classic Madonna tune. I knew that woman. It was Frankie.

The brilliant and beautiful Frankie Taylor was my ex–
personal trainer and current forever friend. We had met in her
Nineties Pop Princesses dance class. Not only did I love her
energy, attitude, and choreography, but she bore an uncanny
resemblance to a young Lorelai from *Gilmore Girls*. Lorelai
Gilmore was probably the only person in the world I would
allow to force me to do burpees.

Frankie was of average height but has the kind of slim,
athletic figure that seems effortless. Her light eyes were always
sparkling with a joke or embarrassing, hilarious story. She never
broke my cardinal rule of fitness training (never, ever tell me I
have only two reps left and then say "Just five more!" because I
will kill you). She was irreverent and fun, ambitious even when
she doubted her own abilities, and a solid and loyal trainer
who had killer taste in music (1970s, '80s, and '90s, with the
occasional early-2000s jam thrown in for good measure).

I pressed "see more" to expand the caption. Frankie was running free online fitness classes on Instagram. *GLOWING LIVE
HQ*, it said, *aka Frankie's living room*, which made sense. I
could spy her sofa just out of the frame. *We are loving bringing all the retro fitness funtimes to you.* It was followed by at
least six enthusiastic emojis.

I wasn't sure what did it—the song or the colors or the
jumping jacks (an exercise I despise, because after having
children, it was impossible to do them without peeing a little).
Maybe it was the sound of Frankie's voice, with her North
London lilt, that triggered a memory of a happier time, a time
when my hips did more than just expand; they shook and
shimmied. I missed dancing. I missed exercising. I needed to
get my ass up off the sofa and try something new.

I woke up the next morning resolved to stop moping around
and drowning my sorrows in chardonnay and shortbread. I

put on my sneakers and four layers (spring in Scotland is still basically winter anywhere else) and went for a run for the first time in at least five years. I never liked running, which must have been invented by a flat-chested person, and it was more of a walk, and my knees creaked the whole way, but it felt good—damn good—to be outside my house and move my body for a little bit.

High on endorphins, I put a documentary on for the kids with the instruction to "watch this and tell me ten new facts you learned," my go-to assignment for when I needed time to work or think or both. And I decided, with my face still bright red like a tomato, to reboot the internship project once more.

On my computer, I had saved an original longlist of dream jobs from shortly after my night with Laura and Rebecca at the Coral Room. In the midst of an interminable lockdown, not a lot seemed feasible. Not only was Christie's a nonstarter, but the rest of the art world was out too. Museums and galleries were closed, with no opening date on the horizon, and most staff had been furloughed. Restaurants and hotels were also on my list, but again, nothing was open and people who were actually in the industry were struggling to figure out how to stay afloat or being laid off. Then there were my wild cards: Disney (closed), marine biology (fish present, institutes closed), and teaching (haha, just kidding).

But one option increasingly seemed to make sense. I had never really taken it seriously as a professional prospect, considering it only briefly as a fun side hustle perhaps, but now, during the pandemic, it seemed to be booming: the fitness industry.

I did not come from athletic stock. Back in Miami, Saturdays were devoted to the holy trinity of beer, nachos, and the Florida Gators, and Sundays were for penance (watching the

Miami Dolphins lose). But no one in my family had ever even played football, except if it was on a video game. Once, we caught my brother Ted running in a hunched-over position, his torso parallel to the ground. When pressed as to why, he told us it was a more aerodynamic position. He could not figure out why Olympians had not yet adopted it.

Like them, I have terrible balance and even worse hand-eye coordination and would be unable to reliably hit a ball with a bat, racket, or club if my life depended on it. But I always loved to dance, and more than that, I loved the whole concept of being part of a team or group. I originally joined a local cheerleading squad because it was the cool thing to do—all the popular girls did it, and I was desperate to be one of them. But then it turned out that I loved the friendship, the camaraderie, the pom-poms, the swishy skirts, and, a few years later, the fact that cheerleading allowed for PG-13 canoodling with boys because it was easy to sidle up next to them on the bus during away games. I loved the social element of it—waxing our legs in the locker room while we gossiped about our teachers, and going to sleepovers after big games, where we gossiped about crushes—and I loved feeling physically strong. Like I could handle anything. Like I could live forever.

Cheerleading was my gateway drug into other forms of dance and fitness that continued into adulthood. I was a sucker for any new trend, the weirder the better. My constant thirst for novelty and my "I'll try anything once" attitude meant that, with the notable exception of goat yoga (literally yoga with goats), I had tried more fitness trends than I can even list. But I'll try to:

- pole dancing
- cardio striptease

- aerial yoga
- Bikram yoga
- other non-Bikram hot yoga
- cold or room-temperature yoga
- Zumba (I was an early adopter in Miami, before it became a global phenomenon)
- every type of dance, including but not limited to Latin, hip-hop, belly, Bollywood, tap (a beginners' community college course, age thirty-five), ballet (a beginners' class at nineteen, attended by women over the age of sixty and me), jazz, musical theater jazz, Jazzercise, really anything involving jazz hands
- barre
- Pilates (mat and, when I feel like exercising while lying down, reformer)
- HIIT
- all manner of boot camps (*not* a fan of being yelled at)
- Couch to 5k (I did succeed in running a 5k eventually, in forty-nine minutes, so I basically walked it)
- anything with the word "cycle" in it (1Rebel Cycle, Groove Cycle, SoulCycle, Psycle)

But in spite of my varied and extensive experience, fitness had never been more than a hobby. Sure, I loved the physical act of getting sweaty, listening to great music, and moving my body with gratitude that it worked, especially as I got older and things worked less well than they once might have. A few times in my life, I had toyed with the idea of making it less of a hobby and more of a commitment—training as a Zumba instructor or a yoga teacher—but it never made it beyond the New Year's resolution phase. The idea of teaching a class where I was the one in control of the moves and the playlist sounded entertaining, but other obligations always took priority. And just like with theater, a tiny, steely voice inside of me reminded me that I was afraid that I wouldn't be fast enough or fit enough to pass muster. Failing Zumba certification felt like an embarrassment I wasn't ready to experience.

(I did however once contemplate the idea of inventing my own yoga "concept," BB Yoga. BB stood for Big Boobs. It would be a place where no woman would ever have to roll back in the plow pose and lie there while her breasts suffocated her face again. *No plow!* That would be our foundational tenet.)

But now, with no viable internship prospect in sight, I reconsidered my previous hesitation. Not many industries boomed during the pandemic, but online fitness was one of them. We had entered, ostensibly, the golden age of dancing in your living room. And sure, I had never really given it serious consideration, but if there was ever any time to see if it was the possible job for me, this was it.

There were added benefits. The endorphin rush I experienced on just one morning walk/run made me feel happier and more optimistic than I had in the month since leaving New York. Maybe I would burn off some of these tiramisu calories that were making my jeans fit so tight. (At least, I assumed they were. I more or less managed to change from "night pajamas" to "day pajamas" each morning, but that was about it.) Who knows—I could end up some thick-hipped, big-boobed, body-confident influencer who inspired women everywhere and made seven figures a year shilling green juice cleanses in Lululemon pants. Stranger things had happened, and just in the past few months.

Most of all, I was desperate and ready to say yes to absolutely anything at that point to keep my internships going. If

I couldn't, it felt as though—both physically and emotionally
—I would crumble under the weight of my despair. And all
the cinnamon buns.

I knew immediately whom to call—my Instagram inspiration, Frankie. Back when she was my personal trainer, she came
to my house weekly, ostensibly to make my muscles stronger
but mostly to chat, which was part of why we got along so
well. Between squats and lunges in my living room we plotted
her future. When we met, she was harboring dreams of setting
up her own fitness brand. As a freelancer, even a successful
one with a following of devoted fans, the cards were stacked
against her. Big studios paid instructors like her an hourly
rate, based on how many people showed up to her classes,
the time of day she was teaching, and her level of seniority.
Since she was a contractor, she wasn't entitled to the benefits
of being a regular employee, like vacation or sick pay. In fact,
if an instructor got sick and couldn't teach a class, not only
did they not get paid, but they had to find their own replace-
ment instructor; if they didn't, they could get blacklisted from
working at that studio and others. Everything was set to favor
the studios or big brands, leaving amazing trainers—even star
ones like Frankie, who attracted a large following—in a pre-
carious professional and financial situation.

Frankie wanted to start a new and different type of fitness company—one with a slick brand that was retro, fun,
and inclusive and supported its teachers and trainers as real
people, not cogs in a machine. She was frustrated with the
business model for the bigger chains, which maximized profit
at the expense of people, and felt there was a better way that
was both commercially viable and fun. During our few years
of weekly workouts, she had spoken about the idea of building her own company. Our personal training sessions very

quickly morphed into business training sessions, with me suggesting plans between planks. Amid crunches and cooldowns, she would plot her strategy, while I would absorb and advise.

In 2018, she launched what eventually became Retroglow Studios, offering retro fitness and dance classes around London supported by a team of attractive, enthusiastic, dynamic instructors. They performed at festivals and events and ran private workshops for bachelorette parties and office fun days. Before the pandemic hit, things had been going very well. A few weeks before I left for New York, we met for burgers (not burpees). I told her about my upcoming internship plans and asked, only half-jokingly, if she might consider hiring me as an intern one day in the future. I said I could help with whatever tasks she needed and come to all of her classes. I was populating my longlist at that point and fitness seemed at least as interesting as being a farmer; plus, free classes.

"Of course, babes," she said, through a mouthful of vegan cheese. "Anytime."

Anytime turned out to be week seven of lockdown. After the kind of day that required hours of sitting under the table (with a large glass of wine, not part of my daughter's strategy but increasingly part of mine), I shot her a text.

OK my love, I have a proposition for you. We had talked before about me possibly interning with you to learn about the fitness industry. Obviously, that was back when classes were in real studios and we could all stand and sweat within two meters of each other. But would you consider taking me on as a virtual intern? (FREE OF COURSE.) I can work for you and help you with whatever you need as you transition into digital fitness. Social media, tech, marketing—you name it, I'll do it. The only thing I can't do is make you actual coffee.

I stared at the three dots that told me she was writing something but not sending it. I held my breath. I had no other options; it was this or days on end of making collages about the solar system.

Her reply zinged back: *Hey boo! So sorry, I'm trying to remember so many things all the freakin time! This could be great ya know! Let's hop on a call.*

A few days later, we got to see each other's faces on Zoom. After exchanging lockdown stories, we got down to it. She'd love to have me as an intern. "But, you should know, I've never had an intern," she confessed.

I told her not to worry. This was my second internship, after all. I was a pro.

To start off, we decided that I should fit in a few tasks around my homeschooling schedule: things I could do on my own time, like creating posts for social media or building and populating a spreadsheet for her that detailed what other fitness studios were offering in terms of virtual fitness—the platforms they were using, the cost, the class options—and then she'd throw me more stuff as she thought of it. We'd also catch up a few times a week on Zoom so I could pick her brain (and, as ended up happening, so she could pick mine).

We also agreed that, to really go the extra mile for industry research, I should take as many different online fitness classes as I could. Within the next few hours, my calendar was full of exciting-sounding appointments with things called VOGA and Disco Barre and gong bath. Not only would I be doing thorough research in order to be an intern who went above and beyond, but it would help me build back some of the physical strength I had lost since lockdown began, and that, in itself, was a big enough reason to do it. Maybe the most important one.

As time ticks on, our bodies age but our brains still think we are capable of doing a split. We all think we're going to age gracefully. Don't deny it—once upon a time, in those lazy, hazy days of your early twenties, when your boobs were pert and your skin was taut, you sat around with your friends after a few drinks (by which I mean cheap vodka diluted with cranberry juice that came in a carton) and said things like "I would never, ever inject rat poison in my face" or "She looks so fake with that face-lift, she should have just let herself get old naturally. That's what I'm going to do."

I'm the first to admit that I was one of those naïve babes. When my mother-in-law told me she got regular "vampire facials" (where they take out some of your face blood, mix it in a centrifuge with Dracula's saliva or something like that, and then *put it back*) I scoffed (internally of course—I may have been naïve, but I didn't have a death wish, which is why I'd never scoff at my truly lovely mother-in-law to her practically juvenile face).

But, eventually, I couldn't outrun the horrors of aging. Not just the wrinkles and my lockdown silver roots but all those signs that my nearly forty-year-old body just didn't bounce back the way it used to and even required the care of a doctor: the time I scratched myself in the cornea with a pine needle while setting up the Christmas tree, the time I sliced open a part of my hand while attempting to wash a wineglass (after drinking the wine in the glass, my bad). The combo of a less supple body and a stubborn disbelief that I couldn't do everything I always had, plus my God-given clumsiness, spelled disaster more than once.

Just over a year before, on New Year's Day, my friend Laura and her family were visiting us in Skye. The day was cold but crisp and sunny as we drove across the island to hike the famous Fairy Pools. Our route took us in the shadow of the snow-covered Cuillin mountains, and we parked at the start of the walk as instructed. After the requisite twenty minutes to disembark our cars (two kids, one dog, one baby, one diaper change, four bathroom breaks), we headed to the start of the walk. "There's a lot of black ice," the parking attendant told me. "Mind your step."

"Did you hear that?" I turned back to everyone, ever the mother hen in these situations. "She said there was a lot of black ice, so watch y—"

I hit the ground, landing directly on my right knee, as I slipped on the ice with impeccable comedic timing. Everyone started fussing but I told them in no uncertain terms that I was totally fine and we should just soldier on. We walked for two hours, my knee throbbing excruciatingly the entire time, but I refused to acknowledge that it was anything more than a bruise. My body was resilient! It could take a little bruise.

When we got home, I sat down for a few hours and then could not get up. It turned out that my little bruise was a partially torn meniscus, and for months afterward, I was on crutches, had physical therapy, and was generally afraid of anything that involved jumping. I was also forced to contend with the fact that my body didn't recover as quickly as it did back in my cheerleading days, when a fall off the pyramid was quickly brushed off, like a speck of dust on our pristine uniforms.

The pandemic had brought my body's frailty into sharp relief. This stupid, tiny germ had shut down the world. People were getting sick and people were dying in huge numbers, vaccines and treatments didn't exist yet, and there was no idea what the endgame might be. I became obsessed with constantly breathing deeply, as if to make sure my own lungs were still functioning and there. I was so tired of feeling weak all the time. If I couldn't control what was happening around me, at the very least I could control my own body. I wanted—needed—to feel strong again. Working with Frankie seemed like the best way to do it, given the current limitations of lockdown.

"You're going to love it," Frankie had said to me right before we hung up. "I think people have fewer inhibitions when they are working out at home. I know I do. I can prance around in a leotard and nobody looks at me weird."

I hung up the call and felt, for the first time in weeks, like I had something to look forward to. Thinking about leg warmers and neon headbands provided an excellent distraction from the chaos mounting inside, and outside, of me.

Chapter 8
The Hot Mess Express

Hi hi hi! I'm just working on your social posts for this week but struggling to figure out which pictures to use. I know they have to be "retro." What would you say is retro, exactly?

I pinged the text quickly over to Frankie. It was 6:00 a.m. and I was trying to schedule the week's worth of Instagram posts before the twins woke up and the day really began. We had gotten into a lockdown routine, which helped a little bit. The days, at least, were predictable, even if they were predictably bad. Every day, I dragged myself out of bed to complete my Retroglow tasks while Carlos made coffee and breakfast. Then the kids started "school" at eight thirty, attending classes on Zoom right in the middle of the dining table. The joy of our "open-plan living space" in Skye meant that this same room was also the kitchen and living room.

Those mornings, I took the lead, observing and assisting during most of the live class sessions, while Carlos locked himself in the office handling work call after work call. Then we swapped around lunchtime, when I worked and he fed the kids. Then back to me after lunch, and in the late afternoons he took over again, making them run around outside for PE and letting them watch TV. After four, I'd do at least one workout, part of my Retroglow market research, and then, before dinner, fill in the market research spreadsheet I had been populating for Frankie. The kids got into bed around eight thirty, ideally without a meltdown (never guaranteed, and it could be by any of the four of us), and then Carlos and I would pour ourselves a large gin and tonic and wine, respectively, stress out about life for the next hour or two, binge-watch something stupid on TV, and fall into bed, only to do it all again the next day.

And the next day. And the next day. Time had become my least favorite kind of trainer, the one that tells us we had only two reps left, only to turn around and say, *"Just five more!"*

Frankie's response to my text was less than enlightening: *Retro! Oof that's hard. Less about a time period and more about subcultures.*

That was Frankie—the most vaguely intellectual fitness visionary ever. I needed specific search parameters for sourcing images from Google that I could use in her Instagram posts. "Subcultures" was not going to cut it—it brought back pictures of goths, heavy metal heads with pink mohawks, and Harajuku girls in plaid skirts and pigtails. *OK, but like what subcultures? Or like time periods?*

Hmm, I guess it can only go back so far. You don't see anything Victorian being described as retro. Catch my drift?

I did not. But eventually, I came up with my own litmus test: Is this something that was cool when I was in middle school (and Frankie in elementary school)? Okay, great. It was "retro" now.

Social media was an integral part of Frankie's business, so it was a key piece of my internship. Social was the main way of attracting new members to the Retroglow family; in fact, with the world having moved online during the pandemic, it was the only way. The landscape was changing rapidly. Retroglow had to differentiate itself among the cacophony of new studios in the virtual fitness world that had popped up since the pandemic began; the market was getting saturated.

Luckily, the potential client pool had grown even faster. Now that Frankie was no longer confined to a dance studio in East London, anyone anywhere in the world with a broadband connection, a set of hand weights (or two cans of beans), and a bright green leotard (optional) could be a Retroglow member and take classes any time of day from the comfort of their home.

My job was to prepare a week's worth of social media posts and send them to Frankie for her edits and feedback. This was the holy grail of intern tasks, perfectly designed for young twentysomething interns who know their TikTok from their Twitch (two words I had to Google). At forty, I needed to acquire some new skills. You'd assume I might have been good at this—after all, I was one of Facebook's first two thousand users, but back then I mainly used it to track where my latest crush's classes were and then accidentally show up.

My first few posts for Retroglow were disastrous and required a lot of editing. Over the weeks, Frankie patiently instructed me on how to write the right kind of Instagram caption to attract as many followers as possible, hoping that would convert them into clients enrolling in classes. The studio had a strong brand voice—a sassy, supportive, cheeky Londoner who was super-cool and happy to welcome you into her bubble. Basically, it was Frankie's voice—one so unique to her, it wasn't easy to mimic.

For example, posts where body parts were glorified ("check out those rock-hard abs!") were a no-go; she didn't want anything included that would make people feel like they were trying to reach an unattainable level of perfection and she was sensitive about touting a particular body image. Or once, when I signed off a post with "Yay," she wrote back: *Change that to Super-YAYsies! And it's good to go.*

We mixed images to test what worked best. Some were of her and her photogenic team of instructors dressed in pastels with blow-up palm trees, boom boxes, and flamingos. We posted them alongside photos from the 1970s, '80s, and '90s that were "brand-aligned": Jane Fonda and Cher in tights and high-cut leotards; Grace Jones glamorously stumbling out of a nightclub with one nipple showing; lots and lots of images of the cast of *Saved by the Bell*. Big hair, bright clothes: it was all gloriously "retro," I was told.

I found this task if not intellectually stimulating then well suited to my current state of mind: it required some critical thinking (Seventies Jane Fonda? Nineties Jane Fonda?) but not too much. Embodying Frankie's upbeat attitude did make me feel happier—if I forced myself to smile while drafting the posts, they came out better, and the sheer act of arranging my cheek muscles into that wide curved shape made me feel better too. What I was doing was not rocket science, but it was important—her follower count was growing, which meant her business was growing, and that was our objective.

I was a model intern: responsive, poised, diligent about the tasks I had been assigned, even though it was gradually occurring to me that working in a fitness business was just like working in any other business; the main issues I discussed with Frankie on our check-in calls were about marketing, HR, employment, finance, and lots of other things that were intimately familiar to me. My input, honed from years of experience running my own business, was valuable to her and she was grateful for it. But more than once, I wondered if this was a fitness internship or just my old job with more neon.

Still, I was grateful for the distraction. Spending 24/7 with Carlos and the kids had taken a toll. Sometimes I would go sit in the car alone in the driveway just to get out of the house. But more often than not, I relied on my tasks for Retroglow to keep my head above water—especially the ones that involved taking classes from all her competitor studios. This "market research" was absolutely, hands-down the best thing about that entire internship and probably the best thing about that strange period of my life.

Frankie had asked me to help her understand the new Wild West of online fitness by reviewing the content being generated by other fitness providers. We put together a list of comparable brands. Most were London-based at first—those she would have considered her competitive market when classes were happening in person—but that expanded as every Tina or Tony from around the world started to offer their own online exercise experience. Each brand went into my spreadsheet, where I wrote out the basics neatly across the columns: type of offering; type of membership and fees; messaging used to describe their online offering (e.g., Was it short-term? Or their plan for the future?); platform used; and things like that. The last column was my favorite: my personal review of the classes. I took at least one session at every single one.

The constant exercise was having the desired positive effect. In spite of living through one of the most challenging times in human history, I was on an endorphin rush, like, all the time.

Once the posting was done, the rest of my daily tasks took place on the living room carpet. I sprawled out on my rug, trying classes from Sydney to Sacramento and everywhere in between. Some were weirdly wonderful, and some were just weird. I reviewed Retrosweat, an Australian fitness concept that took the idea of eighties nostalgia to a new level. I diligently reported back to Frankie:

> In an unironic hot-pink leotard and matching leg warmers, and a mega blond wig, instructor Shannon Dooley looked like my California Dream Barbie come to life. She pranced around the hot-pink studio, complete with its own vanity table and life-size glittery unicorn. It was a lot, but also just enough. Fantastic production value, great screen resolution, rocking '80s soundtrack and the feeling that I was eight years old again, wearing a side ponytail and lying on my New Kids on the Block bedsheets.

Fitness professionals were getting creative with their offerings, and not always to great effect. House of VOGA, for example, a popular in-person workout in London, offered a combination of voguing and yoga that was, besides being total cultural appropriation, totally bizarre. I wrote:

> For a start, why does everyone on staff have VOGA names? Julia was "Juju," Alyssia was "Sia." For the purposes of research, I referred to myself as "Sha" in emails with them. There were a number of technical difficulties which made me think none of them were terribly adept at using a computer. All in all, would not take again.

Other classes you could tell were awesome in person—in dark rooms with flashing lights and sweaty bodies—but did not translate very well to the privacy, or distractions, of one's living room. I did one awkward session of VXN, a straight-forward concept: sexy dancing and a lot of touching yourself.

Unsurprisingly, VXN was invented in my hometown of Miami. A few times I had taken a VXN class in person while visiting my parents. And the experience was, as we say in Miami, "so Miami": the kind of dancing we used to do at parties and clubs in high school, only now it was branded and you wouldn't get detention for doing it. The moves had names like "Ridin Round and Gettin It," "Sex Bombs," and my personal favorite, "Milkshakes."

In-person VXN classes were so much fun, with amazing cardio and a definite "vibe"—sultry, with a sweat-induced humidity and music too loud to hear yourself think. You could really *feel* the bass line. But it was difficult to re-create that sexy magic at home in my living room, groping myself in broad daylight. It was hard to hear Beyoncé over the children running around the house screaming, "CAN YOU HEAR ME NOW, OVER," on their new walkie-talkies. I actually had to stop when I almost gave the mailman a heart attack as he dropped off a package while I was midtwerk.

Gong baths also suffered online, as I noted when I took a class from one of Retroglow's competitor studios. Gong bath is based on lying down with your eyes closed, listening to someone play Tibetan bowls or, hence the name, a gong. It stretched the definition of fitness, but the class was listed in the studio's fitness section, so as far as I was concerned, it counted.

Gong bath experts claim that the vibrations of the gong are meant to create unity between your brain waves and the gong. I have no idea if that is scientifically proven, but I can vouch for the fact that I left previous in-person gong baths feeling like I had just eaten a pan of pot brownies.

Lying on my bedroom floor in my virtual gong bath, I felt less than Zen. Once again, house noise abounded. I tried my best to relax as the meditation began. Through the laptop, the instructor told me to "say your affirmations with your hand on your heart center: I love myself. I believe in myself." There was a third one, but I couldn't hear what it was over my husband yelling at the twins to quiet down because mommy was relaxing upstairs.

There were moments when, breathing deeply on the floor of my bedroom, I did feel calmer. But then the internet connection went patchy. "We must celebrate the microwaves," I thought I heard, as the instructor cut in and out. Through the tinny speakers of my laptop, the gong sounded less like it was sending out reverberations to pass over me like the crest of a wave and more like the ringing of an annoying little bell, the kind that a character played by Maggie Smith would use to call her servant in a period drama. Once again, I was foiled— my dog pushed the door open, lay down next to my head, and started snoring. Soon, she had drowned out the gong and it was a lost cause.

In addition to doing the market research, I was taking at least two or three of Frankie's classes each week. Just over a month of interning with Retroglow had made my body more able to cope with the brutal workouts she doled out.

Beneath her energetic, enthusiastic "we got u, babes" veneer lived a hard-core taskmaster/sadist. How many walking lunges could one normal, red-blooded person be expected to do? Her classes were like oatmeal-raisin cookies—on the outside, you might mistake them for chocolate chip, but once you took a bite, it was clear it was misery masquerading as joy, pain pretending to be pleasure. Did I mention I hate raisins?

Despite my constant yelling in disbelief at the screen (*Dear god, another set of mountain climbers, have we not suffered enough?*), by week four of my internship, I was actually able to do the mountain climbers without falling flat on my face or quitting halfway through the track. It felt good. While I'm a big proponent of loving yourself at any size, it was nice that my pajama pants (I still hadn't attempted jeans) fit looser. My biceps were defined, and you could even see my triceps if I flexed really, really hard and you squinted. Somewhere, deep down underneath the layer of belly fat, I'm absolutely certain there was a six-pack.

Taking eight to ten workout classes per week also helped with another pandemic-induced problem: mild panic attacks. I was worried about my aging parents, so far away in Miami and in complete denial that they were high-risk. I was worried that schools would never reopen and that I'd be destined to live my life as a failing schoolteacher, my children growing up unable to master basic grammatical concepts and blaming me for their inability to get a job or, you know, do long division. I was worried I would never figure out what I wanted to do with the rest of my life, or that maybe I would but it wouldn't matter because I would never, ever be able to leave my house.

My bedroom was in what was basically a loft, with Velux windows on the roof that opened out to a view above the trees and, on a clear day (so, once a month in Scotland), a view of the mountains. It had become my meltdown spot. Every time an attack hit, I unbolted the windows and stuck my head outside, no matter the weather. The glass pane would shelter me from the worst of the rain (it was usually rain), but the wind knew no such parameters and would blow in on my face from all sides. I barely noticed. I tried to breathe. My mind was racing, my face wet with tears.

I was scared, worried, sad. On top of all that, I felt resentful and then, in that familiar vicious loop, guilty about being resentful. Every conversation or catch-up with friends or family went the same way: "How are you?" "Oh, fine really, I mean, we're so fortunate compared to so many others that I can't really complain, can I?"

But the thing is, I did want to complain. I wanted to yell and scream and pout and cry. Of course, I couldn't do that. It would be tone-deaf, immature, and ungrateful. So I led with gratitude on the outside. But on the inside I was screaming.

This was supposed to be my goddamn time. I shouldn't be here. I should be backstage at *Assassins* helping the actor-musicians with their instrument swaps or in a back room at Christie's appraising a Lee Krasner painting. I was supposed to be resolving my inner turmoil, not falling deeper and deeper into it. I was supposed to be able to escape.

And then of course, I felt even more awful—selfish, ungenerous, spoiled. I was well fed and well rested, with money and a job and my health. The world was burning down around me and I was worried about my lack of adventure and midlife crisis. If a pandemic couldn't help this be enough for me, maybe no number of internships could.

As the frozen Scottish air blasted me in the face, reality and logic finally came flowing back in. I had to suck it up. I had to be strong. I had to make it through the next day, and the next one.

The workouts helped with my ability to cope with that; every day I got stronger mentally too. And while it was nice to see someone more toned in the mirror, it was even better to not feel like a total basket case teetering on the verge of anxious outbursts all the time. I had taken a Peloton boot camp class the week before as part of my research, and with Lady

Gaga blaring in the background and sweat pouring down my face, I held a plank for longer than I thought humanly possible. Cody (my favorite instructor), all handsome chiseled jaw and sassily raised eyebrow, looked right at the camera (or, perhaps, directly into my soul) and said: "Girl, fix your wig. It is time to get off the hot mess express."

It stuck with me. I had absolutely been riding in a first-class cabin on the hot mess express, but now, thanks to Frankie and her team of brawny co-instructors, I felt, if not completely together, then at least less weak, less powerless. I was stronger and maybe even more capable.

Before, if I was tired or hungover or both, I used to blow off class. Now exercise was my job and I *had* to show up because I needed to report back to Frankie. And even though I started out each warm-up thinking, "Maybe I'll just do the first ten minutes and stop for another coffee," by the time I reached the fourth set of squats, genuinely wanting to kill someone and/ or die myself, I was willing myself to keep going for one more eight count. At the very end when we cooled down, I would feel, honestly, freaking amazing. For at least a few hours.

I realized, as I sped through my "around the world in eighty workouts" agenda, that Frankie wasn't just a good teacher; she was a great one. I was amazed by her ability to create entertaining, engaging, and exciting experiences, even though just like the rest of us, she had plenty of days where she felt like crap. Sometimes we'd be talking just before a class and she'd have a terrible migraine; twenty minutes later, she'd be in mint-green Lycra leggings with a headband around her head, telling us a story about the first time a boy touched her boob to a song by Take That, as we held a deep plié.

I knew I probably should be watching and observing like I did in New York, to learn about the ins and outs of this profession: taking notes on Frankie's teaching strategy to understand what she did or didn't do, what I liked and disliked, or what I would incorporate into my own teaching method. But as a result of my internship, I had been coming to realize that maybe fitness wasn't my permanent career path.

Any dreams I had of using this opportunity to apprentice as a teacher were dashed early on, when I realized that I couldn't just paint some glitter on my eyelids, turn on my phone camera, and actually teach a class. Frankie and her team were experienced and certified in "Exercise to Music," a formal qualification. They knew not just what your muscles were called (What is a trapezius? I still don't know) but also how to help people prevent injury. This was even more important when you couldn't see the people following along with your movements.

Teaching would require training, and I wasn't sure if I was ready to make that commitment after lockdown ended, or ever. But maybe that is what real interns are supposed to figure out. They try something. They like it, or hate it. Sometimes it's horrible and not right for them. Sometimes it's wonderful but still not right for them (see: my own experience at *Ocean Drive*). For me, figuring out what I didn't want to do was as valuable as finding something I did.

Even more valuable was how both my internships had relieved me of my duty to perform. Both in the theater and in fitness, I wasn't expected to know everything, or even much of anything. The pressure to be the best, or even just to keep things afloat—to make sure that a scene ran perfectly or a budget was balanced correctly—belonged to my bosses, not me. I hadn't even realized how much the sheen of perfectionism, which I had diligently painted on every morning since I could remember, had begun to crack, until I didn't have to wear it anymore. Even as a consultant, it was important to get dressed up for clients and to look and act the part. I was paid to be the expert, brilliant, emotionally stable, problem-free version of me. Not the deodorant-stained-top-that-you-tried-to-rub-out-with-spit one.

Though I knew I'd probably have to put that suit of perceived perfection back on again one day, I was relishing the chance to have a little break from it, to learn from someone else, and to do what I was told for a while, without having to be the person on whose shoulders lay success or failure.

The end of my internship coincided with the beginning of summer, and with it, what we all hoped would be brighter times. The days had gotten longer, the snow had melted off the peaks of the distant hills, and my broom tree, barren and brown for eleven months of the year, had exploded into a glorious yellow burst of color. The kids' school in London emailed to say that they wanted to bring them all back together in person for the final week of school, for social activities and "assessment tests" (what would undoubtedly be the surest indictment of my incompetence at homeschooling). Vaccine trials had begun and a "road map" out of lockdown was in development. The pandemic was far from over, but it seemed like perhaps this phase of it was coming to an end.

The final few weeks had cemented my assumption that fitness was definitely not going to be my next career. Many parts of it had been deeply fun, especially in the midst of a dark time. I credit Frankie and Retroglow for pulling me out of what could have been a very deep hole of despair. Many days just knowing there was that Britney vs. Whitney aerobics class waiting for me at the end of the day was enough of a distraction to keep the demons at bay, at least for forty-five minutes.

But ultimately it wasn't the job for me. The teaching bit, while still intriguing, didn't seem like it would ever be my passion. (Although it could, perhaps, be a great hobby, so watch this space for BB Yoga coming to a studio near you!) And watching Frankie over the last months, it was clear that teaching and brainstorming fun class ideas and making epic themed playlists was only a small part of the job. Most of her work was running a business. That was familiar, too much so. The whole point of this internship effort was to find something that would push me out of my comfort zone. Since having the twins, I hadn't done that enough. Or, really, at all. And while I was super-comfortable in my comfort zone, wearing leggings to work, I wasn't growing (except for my glutes). And that was the problem. My next internship, whatever it was, needed to stretch me intellectually, not just physically.

On my last day as her intern, Frankie was so sweet and emotional. *U have been unreal,* she texted me. *It has opened my eyes as to what else I should do to help my business grow. Thank u for believing in me!* Three heart emojis and one party face.

Before I signed off, I had one last task: scheduling the week's social media posts. I pulled up a photo of Kage, one of Frankie's sexiest instructors, in gold hot pants. He would be teaching an eighties *Saturday Night Fever* aerobics class that week. *WOO,* I wrote. *It's time for some banging tunes with Retroglow online this week! We got u babes and we are feeling good about what's ahead!* And, I think for the first time in a long time, I really meant it.

Chapter 9
Rebel Without a Cause

On the morning that altered the entire course of my professional life, I ran into the cavernous Turbine Hall at the Tate Modern, dripping wet from the rain with a fierce hangover, fifteen minutes late for my meeting with Nigel, a junior member of the Tate's curation team. I was twenty-one years old. The meeting had been orchestrated by one of my art history professors back in the States. I had fallen in love with art history and had added it as a joint major, along with women's studies.

I had a lot riding on this interview and was kicking myself for being late, a result of a long evening of partying that ended in line for a Big Mac at 4:00 a.m. the night before. It was my last year of college and my visit to London was an attempt to figure out what I wanted to do after graduation. The Tate interview was one of two I had set up that day, with grand hopes that someone would be so delighted by my wit, intelligence, and personality that they'd offer me a job with a UK visa, which I needed to work in the country.

When I had come to London to study abroad during the spring semester of my junior year, I enrolled as a visiting student in University College London's art and architecture program and experienced for the first time in my life the richness, expansiveness, and sheer volume of art available in Europe. All of my classes that semester were "on-site," meaning we either walked around different neighborhoods of the city looking at statues and buildings or met in one of London's many museums to be lectured on paintings as we closely examined them in real life.

I was fascinated by art history in the classroom, but once I went to the UK and experienced the difference of seeing a two-hundred-year-old painting not in a book but on a wall in front of me, noting the brushstrokes, the texture of the paint, the faintest lines where you might see a wisp of a previous draft, it made it feel a lot less like history and a lot more like it could be my future.

London—where I now knew I wanted to live—was both dreamy and impossible. I didn't have a network or even the faintest idea where to start, especially when I didn't have British citizenship. The interview with Nigel was my first contact with the art world. Actually, he was my only contact in the art world. I ran inside the Tate, not stopping for even a moment to marvel at the industrial, postmodern beauty of the museum itself, which had opened only a few years earlier. I took the escalator steps two at a time to the café and found a man that had to be Nigel. He was alone, wearing trendy eyeglasses and with a peeved look on his face.

"Oh my gosh, I'm so, so sorry," I said, peeling off my wet layers, smoothing my frizzy hair, and hoping that the makeup I had plastered on to cover the bags under my eyes had not washed off.

"It's fine," he said, which, when said by a British person, meant it was definitely not fine.

I turned up the charm to maximum, trying to overcome our rocky start. Hangover or not, I was there to sell myself. Of the many museums in London that I would have liked to work at, the Tate Modern was my first choice by a large margin. While I loved the beauty and history of the Old Masters, the tactile nature of the Impressionists, and the weirdness of surrealism, it was contemporary art, especially feminist art and art of political movements, that really got my juices flowing.

The Tate had the best collection in the UK. It also had, at the time, one of the most inclusive approaches to access and museum education and was really focused on how to make sure everyone in the neighborhood felt welcome within its doors. As someone who grew up with parents who assumed that "fifteen minutes at the Louvre would be enough to see everything, what do you mean you need more time?" this was an interest of mine too.

I was particularly interested in the education department, the division of a museum team that would focus on bringing the community in to engage with and learn about the art. I gave Nigel my winningest smile and delivered my spiel: I was dedicated, enthusiastic, and a hard worker. I had interesting and important things to say about art, a subject about which I was deeply passionate. I would take any opportunity—just a chance to get my foot in the door.

"Ha," he said and laughed dryly. "Good luck."

He then proceeded to go on a tirade about his own chosen profession. Was it the rain that made him so fervently angry? My tardiness? The lingering scent of McDonald's fries from the night before? I'll never know. But the message was clear: stay away, little girl. This field is cutthroat, he told me. Everyone was looking for an opportunity to do exactly the thing that I wanted to do, and few ever opened up. Junior curatorial wannabes were like predators at the watering hole, fighting over a few scraps.

Plus, he went on, even if I somehow managed to claw my way to the top of the food chain and emerged victorious with a job offer in hand, the chances of getting someone to sponsor my visa, in this chronically underfunded profession, were "not great" (in British speak, which meant I had a snowball's chance in hell).

I thanked him for his time and left. To say I was deflated was an understatement. I was devastated. The only door I had to the art world had slammed in my face. I walked down the South Bank of the Thames, the rain having stopped by this point, and crossed Waterloo Bridge. The rarely seen British sun was poking through. Cheer up, London was saying, we're not done yet.

The London School of Economics, also known as LSE (which Americans always say stands for "Let's See Europe"), was my fallback plan. It offered a master's degree program in gender studies. Another year of school—that I had to pay for—wasn't the most appealing idea, but I was willing to try anything for that precious visa.

I arrived on time (!) and was ushered into the office of Anne Phillips, the head of LSE's Gender Institute. I hadn't been sure whom I was going to be meeting that day, but I certainly didn't think it would be Anne Phillips. *The* Anne Phillips. Anne Phillips had written some of my favorite works on feminist political theory. I was geeking out.

My two meetings that day could not have been more different. Anne served me warm tea in a beautiful china cup and gave me the hard sell. Come to the LSE! she beckoned. The next year was going to be the first of their newly launched

Gender, Development, and Globalization master's program. I could be one of the first students, help shape the curriculum. The faculty was unparalleled in their knowledge, the class-mates top of their fields from around the world.

It was a no-brainer. The art door was closed, and so I walked through another.

Years later, I thought back to that gloomy 2003 day on a regular basis. What would have happened if I hadn't gone out the night before? If I had sensibly gone home and gone to bed, woken up early, left myself plenty of time to make it to the Tate, owned a better-constructed umbrella (or any umbrella), shown up on time, and found Nigel in a better mood? What would my life have looked like when I hit forty?

Maybe I really belonged in the art world. Maybe I had blown my own destiny back then. Maybe, after five grueling months of lockdown, it was time to find out.

The prime minister declared July 19, 2020, Freedom Day; the UK had bent the COVID curve downward enough that he removed all restrictions and life was "back to normal." I truthfully didn't believe for a second that it would be anything like normal, but it appeared we didn't need to hole up in our rural retreat in Skye any longer. We moved back down to Lon-don, and I went back to the internship drawing board once again, seeing if I could finally figure out which version of my life was supposed to be mine.

········

Back before I left for my Broadway internship in New York, I had been working my network to secure a museum or gallery internship. In spite of turning off that path after col-lege, I had amassed quite a few social contacts in London's art scene. One friend offered to make an introduction for me to someone she knew at Christie's, the renowned auction house, which was where I found myself, wearing my most business-like black dress, at a job interview on a blisteringly cold day in London in February 2020, right before I left for Broadway.

Christie's main sale room in London is on King Street in the St. James neighborhood, so close to Buckingham Palace that if it was completely silent, you could hear the Queen's guards clicking their boots together as they paraded back and forth. The building, home to the famous auction house since 1823, looks like a classic wedding cake on the outside: layered, white, and rich.

When you stepped inside, it was clear the lobby, too, was designed to make you feel important, powerful, and in the mood to drop a cool million on a tea set once owned by Queen Victoria. On that morning when I walked through the doors to persuade someone to give me an unpaid internship, I didn't feel important or powerful—but I was prepared to drop £5.25 on two cappuccinos.

I gave my name at reception and sat down in the waiting area. The woman next to me was wearing a suit and nervously fidgeting with the black leather portfolio she held on her lap, which no doubt contained her résumé. I had not brought my résumé with me. And, hold up, was I supposed to wear a suit? I didn't even own a suit; I hadn't been on a job interview in almost a decade.

I'd never considered working in an auction house, focusing my hunt mainly on museums and galleries, but those were not panning out as I had hoped. The auction house world was one I knew little about, and my assumption was that the few internships available were reserved for children of big buyers and big spenders, not for grown adults whose parents bought their art at Bed Bath & Beyond. But the week before, when my friend had asked me over lunch if I'd like an introduction to her contact, I replied, "Sure, why not?"

A few days later, an email from Arabella, a junior specialist in the Post-War and Contemporary Art Division at Christie's, dinged in my inbox. She had received my details from her boss, who had received my information from our mutual friend, and asked me to come in and see her to discuss a potential three-week work experience.

Originally, my heart had been set on interning in an exhibition space, but the more I thought about it, the more an auction house seemed like an ideal place to learn the ropes. I'd still be able to spend lots of time with art itself—Christie's boasted several galleries and showrooms within its walls, a few of which were open to the public—but I could also learn about the commercial side of the business, something I wouldn't have the chance to do at a museum. My knowledge of how art was bought and sold was gleaned predominantly from films like *The Thomas Crown Affair* or absurdist news about $120,000 bananas duct-taped to walls. If I did want to use this internship as a stepping stone to a real job in the art industry (one that actually paid me money), finding something that built on my existing business experience was probably my best bet.

Once at Christie's I felt increasingly convinced that an auction house was the right idea. The atmosphere in the lobby was buzzing. People came and went in expensive suits, or with designer handbags, or both; some had a studied disheveledness and three-day-old stubble which screamed, "I'm an artist! Look at me!"

Yes, I thought to myself, this could be amazing. It was glamorous for sure, but I had no shortage of meeting fancy people in my real job—in fact, I was pretty sure that many of the philanthropists I had worked with were also Christie's clients. But I didn't care about the buyers as much as the chance to be around artists and, crucially, actual art. It was visual and creative and tactile and real, dealing in physical pieces of painting and sculpture, not just emails and strategies and PowerPoint decks. It was new and different and I had never done it—that is probably what made it most exciting above all else.

A willowy, young, blond woman came out from behind the "employees only" area. She, like so many of the women around us, looked effortlessly stylish in a black turtleneck and plaid wool pants. I made a mental note to buy a few black turtlenecks; it seemed like the unofficial dress code.

"Alisha?" she said, looking at both suit lady and me. I got up and greeted her. If she was surprised at my age, she didn't show it. We sat down on high stools at the lobby's in-house coffee bar (score another point for Christie's).

"I'm so sorry I look so tired, but we've just finished our latest catalog and I've been working several late nights," Arabella said.

She didn't look tired to me—she had the dewy skin of one's early twenties and an accent that betrayed an upbringing almost definitely surrounded by non–Bed Bath & Beyond art. A waiter brought over two coffees and, after taking a sip, Arabella asked, "So, why would you like to come work at Christie's?"

I may not have had a scented copy of my résumé with me, but this question, at least, I was prepared for. I launched into my well-rehearsed speech: midlife crisis, always wanted to work in the art industry, now's my chance to explore, yada yada yada. "Well, I know it sounds quite unusual," I finished. After more than a decade in the UK, I had mostly kept my strong American accent, but something about being around super-posh people always made me sound like Madonna during her British phase. "But I just want to reiterate that I'm happy to do anything. Quite literally anything—file files, transport paintings, get coffees—"

"Oh no, heavens no," she interrupted me. "We have a policy here that we never ask interns to get coffee. We don't do that anymore." Then she leaned in and lowered her voice conspiratorially. "You know, Anne Hathaway actually interned at Christie's in New York to prepare for her role in *The Devil Wears Prada*. But don't worry—things have changed a lot since then."

That was a shame. I had been looking forward to at least one authentic Anne Hathaway experience, but I was excited nonetheless. After a few minutes of banter, Arabella asked when I'd like to start.

"You mean I've got the job?" I exclaimed.

Arabella laughed, "Yes, of course—this wasn't an interview. After all, it's an unpaid work experience."

I shook her hand goodbye and told her I'd see her in May 2020.

But just a few short months after that February day, everything changed in an explosive and unpredictable way. Deep down, I knew the probability of my Christie's internship ever happening was dwindling day by day, but I didn't want to admit it to myself. In April, I heard from Arabella that my internship would be postponed. Postponed wasn't canceled. I went ahead and twerked my way through my internship with Frankie and Retroglow but continued to check in with Arabella. May, June, and July came and went on the calendar. By the summer, some galleries and museums had started to reopen, cautiously and on a limited-entry basis, with prebooked, timed tickets. The art world was coming out of its enforced hibernation, albeit slowly.

Back in post-lockdown life, my panic attacks were less frequent, as the harshest rules of lockdown started to recede; it even seemed like schools would open again in the fall. But the art world wasn't quite ready to do the same, and the auction house offices remained closed. *I'm so sorry*, Arabella wrote in her final email to me. *We are only operating the building at 40% capacity and don't have any idea when work experiences might start again.*

There was no one to blame; like everyone else, the art industry was finding its murky way through the pandemic. In the never-ending age of COVID, midlife interns, or any interns, were not a priority.

I was despondent, but I knew that giving up would only make me feel worse. I wanted this internship, badly; emotionally, I didn't think I could wait a year for it to happen. I had already managed to complete two internships in the strangest of circumstances. Now was not the time to give up. I blasted out my résumé again and sent cold email introductions to any gallery in London that had ever, at any point in the prior decade, advertised for an intern, and I engaged in proactive digital stalking of everyone I had ever met in the art world to see if they would have a call with me so I could "pick their brains."

I knew I couldn't be choosy, and anyway, wasn't I supposed to be getting out of my comfort zone? Figuring it would be better to have any opportunity, even if it didn't fit squarely in the "art" box, I sent off my application for an unpaid weekend volunteer position at the Vagina Museum (*at left, observe this glittery, bloody tampon sculpture as a classic piece of postmodern vulvic expressionism*). Luckily, there wasn't enough time for *them* to reject me too, before an email from Harry Blain appeared in my inbox. "I'd love to see you," he said, "and your timing is great; if you're interested, perhaps you'd like to intern with me? I'm setting up a new business and it should be fun."

Harry Blain had been the first person I emailed when I was seeking an internship in the art world. He was a successful art dealer and entrepreneur turned gallery owner. We had met for lunch in late 2019, at a tucked-away sushi restaurant in the tony Mayfair area of London, the sort of place that accommodates a crowd of masters of industry and their mistresses—intimate, with hidden corners and surreptitious booths, perfect for doing deals of all sorts. I drummed my fingers nervously on the table and checked the time on my phone. I was early—well, not early, really, but on time (for me, early)—and Harry was running late. Ironically, I had been so sure I, too, was going to be late that I had jogged from the Tube, which is why I was sitting there, blotting the sweat from my brow, trying to look calm, cool, collected, and like the kind of person you would want to hire as your intern, when Harry walked in.

We did the British double-cheek kiss and sat down, deciding what to order. I felt too nervous to eat, which, for me, was a new experience. I've never been too *anything* to eat. Within an hour of giving birth to my twins, I was asking for wine and soft cheese. But I was really nervous; to Harry it was just another meeting, sandwiched between others that were undoubtedly more important, but to me it felt like the determination of my future happiness, with a side of miso soup.

As ever, Harry was charming and wonderful. He heard me out, loved the idea, and offered me an internship at his London art gallery, Blain Southern, on the spot. After working in a big museum, being part of a gallery team that also exhibited art to the public was my next best hope. I could already picture it. Soon, I'd be working in a gallery, wearing all black and fake glasses, explaining to a viscount or marchioness that Mickey Mouse breastfeeding from the Queen was really a nuanced metaphor about the postcolonial hegemonic takeover of popular cinematic culture.

A few months later, in the first week of 2020, I had a meeting scheduled with Harry at his gallery to discuss my upcoming internship. I checked in with one of the two ice princesses sitting behind the desk, who were dressed in head-to-toe black. "I'm here to see Harry," I said, picturing myself bringing this girl a black Americano that she'd reject for being too cold. "I'm going to be interning here," I couldn't resist adding. I could feel it in my bones—this was where I was meant to be, whether she thought so or not.

In the midst of my reflections, Harry came downstairs, suggesting we walk around the corner to a little café for a coffee. As we sat down, he apologized: he was so terribly sorry to ruin all my plans but, you see, it looked as though the gallery might be ever-so-slightly going under. They were closing down at the end of the month. The twin ice princesses at the front desk didn't even know yet that they would be out of a job. I comforted him—he had built himself up before and would do it again; I was certain of that and told him so. But I was selfishly disappointed. We parted ways, and I reached out to my art contacts again. Shortly after, I got the opportunity from John Weidman to go to New York, and then the pandemic happened and I hadn't heard from Harry since. Until now.

I had no idea what his new business was, but it was a glimmer of hope and my interest was piqued. We made a date to

meet for coffee at Harry's Notting Hill home for the following Thursday around four thirty. That same evening, I had
seven-o'clock theater tickets for an outdoor, socially distant
production of *Jesus Christ Superstar*, one of my all-time faves,
at the Regent's Park Open Air Theatre. It was the first musical
I was going to see since the fateful *Flying Over Sunset* dress
rehearsal at Lincoln Center six months earlier.

I could not miss it.

But I quickly learned my first art world lesson: plans with
Harry, and in the art world in general, seemed to have a much
more fluid meaning than I was used to. At around three thirty,
just as I was ready to head out the door, I got a text from
Harry. He had been coaxed at the last minute into driving a
few hours outside of London to see a painting, and he thought
he might be late arriving back in; could we meet instead
at five?

I calculated how long it would take me to get from Harry's
house to the theater. It would cut very close to curtain time.
Also, Harry was probably tired after a day of driving. I typed
out a reply: *If it's too much trouble, let's just reschedule.*

But before I sent it, I stopped myself. I was giving him an
out that would be easy for him to take and for this whole
thing to fall apart. Why was I undermining myself? It was
self-defeating. I needed this internship. I had to keep moving.
I deleted the draft and wrote instead: *No worries, let's make
it 5:30. See you then.*

A few hours later, I pulled up in a cab to the front gate
of Harry's house. There were rows of beautiful, five-story-
tall terraced houses, with manicured front entrances and
Maseratis, Ferrari SUVs, and Teslas lined up on the curb, like
a parade of overcompensation. I checked that I had the right
house number, then rang the bell.

The ring was immediately drowned out by the loudest, most incessant barking I had ever heard. The barking got louder and closer until the door handle turned and a very pretty, very pregnant woman opened the door with the cacophonous canine in question right behind her.

That was my first time meeting Rebel, the cockapoo doing all of the yipping and yapping, as well as my first time meeting Maria, Harry's partner. "Hi, hi come in," she said. "Rebel, down. I'm sorry, she's not always like this, Rebel, *down*. Crate, Rebel, crate. *Crate, Rebel.*"

We marched into the kitchen, Maria hushing Rebel, Rebel making her way in the general direction of her crate while continuing to jump on my legs, nip my hands, and bark (this dog could multitask), and me trying to act like I liked this dog who clearly wanted to take a chunk out of my finger.

Eventually, Rebel slunk reluctantly into her crate, which Maria promptly covered with a blanket so my offending face would not cause further panic. Every so often, I'd hear a growl thrown in my direction, fired like a warning shot.

Rebel was the new Carmen. Winning her over would be at the top of my priority list.

Maria made me a passion fruit tea and we talked about the baby on the way, a little girl. This would be Harry's fourth child, but Maria's first, and she was literally glowing. I did not glow when I was pregnant, unless you counted the fact that I was sweaty a lot of the time, and I am always impressed by women who do.

I sat down on the bench in their kitchen next to a neatly folded pile of pastel pink-and-white baby clothes that Maria's mother had recently sent over from Russia. Harry joined us a few minutes later. "In a way, I loved lockdown," he said, when I asked how the last few months had been. It was the first time in years that he hadn't been flying weekly to see clients or artists or both. He seemed refreshed and was excited to tell me about his new business.

Harry had started his career as a dealer—selling art on both the primary market (from artists into the hands of buyers) and secondary market (to and from interested buyers, who were mainly individuals but sometimes galleries)—and he was headed back to his roots. He was starting to deal again, but on "the very high end of the market," he said, working with a small group of collectors and artists with whom he had long-term, trusted relationships.

At least, I think that's what he said. I was barely listening. My heart was racing and it took all of my self-control not to throw my hand in the air like an overexcited kindergartener and scream *Pick me, pick me, pick me!*

Here it was: an actual internship with actual art that didn't seem like it was going to get canceled or go bankrupt or be interrupted by a global pandemic. Harry was working from home at the moment but getting an office space so he could display some of the beautiful works he had in-house. He took me into his living room to show me a few of them. I eyed the clock—I really needed to leave if I was going to make curtain—but I refused to leave until I could seal the deal. Finally, he said the magic words: "So, you see, it's not very clearly defined at this present moment, but would you like to come help me out?"

Inside, I felt like one of those inflatable tube people you see outside car dealerships, frantically waving back and forth and up and down. But I played it cool. "Absolutely," I said. "I've got a month to spare and I'm all yours."

"The only problem is that I may not want to let you go after a month," he said.

"Well, after that you'll have to pay me," I replied, laughing.

I was still walking on air when I got to Regent's Park, where Jesus, Judas, and the apostles were waiting for me (Carlos was there too). It was pouring rain as we sat down, and, since it was an outdoor theater with no roof, I pulled up the hood of my raincoat. A man with a very large mop was sweeping torrents of water off the stage.

Twenty minutes after the scheduled show time, the rain had finally stopped and the performance began. Those first familiar chords were played on the electric guitar, and I felt my heart swell. It had been six entire months since I was behind the scenes on Broadway, but it felt like a lifetime ago. The world had changed so much since then. I had too.

I still dreamed of a career on Broadway, or at least of one behind the scenes, but that wasn't happening anytime soon. This show—outdoors, masked, socially distant—was one of the only ones allowed to run in the UK that summer. New York theaters were still closed, uncertainty was still rampant, and forces far outside my control made it impossible to imagine that I had, in the not-so-distant past, been able to cross a border, alone, easily, not worrying I'd get stuck abroad or sick or worse.

Broadway was on the back burner. Maybe I would have a chance to go back, but who knew how long that would take? I wasn't going to let the internship project stall while I waited for the world to sort itself out. I was excited about this new opportunity, a chance at a job in a field I had always wondered about and loved and that would scratch my itch for novelty and creativity—maybe it was my dream job after all.

The cast filed onto the stage, one by one, wearing masks. At the crescendo of the overture that I've heard a hundred times before, they all pulled down their masks, slowly. Mine stayed on, as the rules required, but underneath, tears were streaming down my face. My first performance since leaving New York felt like coming out of hibernation: a fragile new seed, a promise that something hopeful was ahead.

Chapter 10
Black Turtlenecks and Fake Glasses

The first Monday of September finally arrived. This start date worked very well for me—the twins had started back at school the week before, which gave me a couple of days to get my act together. And by get my act together, I, of course, meant figure out what I was going to wear. In retrospect, I probably should have spent my few weeks of prep time actually, you know, learning more about what contemporary art dealing was, but in my head my wardrobe was the more pressing matter.

I had picked up a few sartorial clues already. All clothing seemed to meet some key criteria: be dark-colored (chic and does not detract from the art), not show too much cleavage (same as previous), and look expensive but not showy (the clothing and the cleavage). Before my Christie's internship was canceled, Arabella had sent me the auction house's formal dress code: *Attire should be professional and appropriate . . . for women, this means tailored skirt or trouser suits with shirt or blouse or smart dresses with a jacket.*

Athleisure was surprisingly not included, and I had never in my life owned a "blouse." The code went on to list the things not considered appropriate: T-shirts, sundresses, shorts, leggings, and flip-flops.

Add hoodies and pajama pants to that list, and it was a full description of every item of clothing I had worn in the past several months.

I was supposed to have had plenty of time to shop for a new, arty wardrobe. After extensive research, I had shortlisted a number of brands that boasted "yoga pants that look like dress pants." But dreams of going on shopping sprees and discovering what a blouse was had been quickly dashed by lockdown and the fact that for all of the spring and most of the summer, I did not change out of actual yoga pants (that looked nothing like dress pants). As September crept up on me, I had yet to figure out what clothing would be required for my not-quite-yet-defined internship for Harry's business that had not quite yet even really launched. I didn't know where I would be going on my first day or what I was going to do. Was I dressing to meet clients or file invoices or hang paintings?

Was I was putting too much emphasis on the wardrobe question? Absolutely. But obsessing over avoiding a fashion faux pas was only the window dressing. I had always been self-conscious about fitting into the art world, since back when I was studying art history in college, in large part because I never felt like I really belonged. People throw around the term "imposter syndrome" a lot, and it's easy to pretend it doesn't exist or that confident people never feel it. But that couldn't be further from the truth. In spite of generally feeling like a boss (having been a boss), there was always a piece of the art world that made me feel like Bridget Jones laughed out of Sunday brunch for wearing a Playboy bunny costume.

When I was growing up, Miami was not the global art metropolis it is now. There was no Pérez Museum, no Wynwood Walls, no Art Basel. Street art was graffiti by someone named Juice on the overpass of I-95. My days were spent at the mall or the beach. The only drawing I engaged in was doodling boys' names in my notebook with hearts and bubble letters. I thought Diebenkorn was an overpriced movie theater snack. I recall my maternal grandparents owning only two paintings—a picture of sad clowns and the classic dogs playing poker—and, on my father's side, my grandmother's walls were plastered with pictures of Jesus, Mary, and any number of saints. My parents' interest was piqued only later in life, after I had left the house and they started buying up everything they could by French contemporary artist Fanch Ledan, whose primary sales outlet was cruise ships.

I signed up for my first college art history class, Female Body Image in French Visual Culture, to fill a requirement and fell in love with art history at first sight. I was fascinated with the idea that you could look and look at something many other people had seen before and discover something entirely new. As a left-brained person, I was attracted to the right-brained-ness of it all. Maybe I was rebelling against my art-free upbringing in the same way that people who were denied junk food as children grow up to eat a Big Mac a day (that is, incidentally, why I'm always so careful to feed my children plenty of junk food).

By the time I reached my junior year, I had taken so many art history classes that I had enough credits to declare it as my joint major. In order to do this, I had to interview with Thomas Batchelder, the undergraduate coordinator for Harvard's History of Art and Architecture Department. Tom was American, but had a faux British affectation (like me when I was nervous, but his came out all the time). I shouldn't have been intimidated by this meeting that was essentially a formality, but I was. To me, it seemed like everyone in the department was polished and vaguely European or from New York's Upper East Side. They wore black turtlenecks, spent their weekends as teenagers at museums instead of bowling alleys, and had been to MoMA (and knew what it stood for). I was convinced that I'd be seen as a phony in their midst; since I couldn't fix my inner insecurity easily, I focused on the outside.

My wardrobe had already gone through a significant metamorphosis since I left Miami for the frigid Boston winters; gone were the backless shirts and open-toed shoes of my youth, replaced by wool sweaters and jeans that didn't have holes in them. But it still wasn't chic enough. Not even sure what I was looking for, I wandered into an Urban Outfitters and found it: a pair of plastic tortoiseshell glasses with clear lenses.

Newly confident in my fake frames, the interview went off without a hitch. Tom was also wearing glasses, and we got along swimmingly. At the end of the meeting he shook my hand and offered me a spot in the program. I was certain it was the glasses; they had fooled everyone into thinking I was a serious art student. I thanked him and turned to go, but he stopped me. "Come, let's take your picture for 'the wall.'"

"The wall" featured Polaroids of all the students who were part of the department. I assumed it was how they told all the black turtlenecks apart from one another when their backs were turned. In my photo, displayed for all to see in the years that followed, I sported my fake glasses, which no one knew were fake. Because it had been immortalized on the wall, I kept up the charade, wearing them to all my art history classes. Ironically, they made it much harder to see. I tried to casually phase them out, but everyone kept asking where they were. Eventually, I told people I had gotten contacts.

Decades later, preparing for my first day with Harry, I still felt a little bit like a charlatan. Even though many years had passed since college, and I was successful in my own right, I wondered if I was crazy for thinking I belonged in the art world. I did not have enough black turtlenecks. Where were those fake glasses when I needed them?

I called my dad for a pep talk. Florida was still reporting high COVID cases but restrictions were almost nonexistent; it was basically a free-for-all.

"Just remember, take your time, do it right, and check your work," he said, which was the thing he had said since I was five, before every first day of school, big test, new job—any activity that required external motivation. But it was hard to hear him over the sound of horns blaring in the background. "Where are you?" I asked.

"We're just at Target. We needed a new garden hose."

"Is that really an essential outing?" I said, sternly.

I could hear my dad rolling his eyes.

"There's nothing else to do. This has been the highlight of our weekend," he said. "Hang on, your mom is grabbing the phone."

"Do you think Harry has any paintings by Fanch Ledan for sale?" my mom chimed in, muffled through two masks. "See if you can get us a good deal."

Sufficiently pep-talked out, I considered my other concerns. I was also intimidated by the complete lack of any structure or plan. The day before I was scheduled to start, Harry phoned to say he actually had to go to Paris for a wedding he had forgotten about—could we push my start date to Wednesday instead?

"By the way, I'm still not sure where our office will be. The place in Mayfair fell through, so I'm looking at a few spots in Notting Hill. I'll text you the details on Wednesday."

"No worries!" I replied, worried; I did not like not having a plan. But hey, I could be spontaneous! I could get out of my comfort zone! I was new and improved, and could do things last minute without getting heart palpitations! Now, someone please grab me a paper bag to hyperventilate into.

I have always been a control freak. I've leveled up since becoming a mom, but I don't think motherhood made me that way. It was always sitting there, disguised in school with titles like "Captain" and "President." "She's a natural leader," nice people would exclaim (the less nice ones just said "bossy"), but they didn't know that my boldness masked a pathological need to always be in charge.

When the twins were born, I was desperate to exert whatever control I could. Nora Ephron famously said that having kids was like throwing a bomb into a marriage, but it was more than that: like a nuclear explosion in my entire life. I kept the twins, and us all, on a rigorous schedule of eating and drinking and sleeping and playtime in order to give me some semblance of order. Only much later did I realize that it was only a facade of control—they were really running the show—but it was the system and the order I needed to make it through the challenging early days.

The pandemic has been terrible for us control freaks, but at least it helped me name the problem. I was not yet an expert at letting go, or anything close to it, but after my Retroglow internship, I was making a concerted effort. I was going to have to get better at being more flexible (and not in the yogic sense) if I was going to survive a month in Harry's world.

Since I had cleared my Monday for now-postponed internship tasks, I threw on a pair of jeans, dropped the kids off at school, and went to meet my friend Kate at Borough Market. It was a sunny September day and I hadn't seen her for months; we were greedy with gossip. Midflow of an important conversation about politics, pandemics, and whether Pop-Tarts were a suitable breakfast for children (I was for; she, against and aghast), my phone buzzed.

It was Harry. He had missed his train and was still in London. *Let's start today, shall we?* he messaged. *Would you mind taking a look at the Art Library to find books on Hockney, Ruscha, and Richter and seeing what was missing? I'll send the login.*

Sounds great, I texted back, with more confidence than I actually felt, given that 85 percent of the instruction had gone over my head. First of all, what was an art library? How would I know what books were missing? How do you even pronounce Ruscha? Was it a *cha* as in cha-cha-cha, or *ska* like the music, or even *sha* like my VOGA name?

I chugged the rest of my coffee, trying not to wince as it scalded my throat on the way down, bid farewell to Kate, and rushed home to stare at my computer screen with no idea of what I was supposed to be doing. I had read somewhere at some point that art books were an important thing, but I could not for the life of me remember why. I was still racking my brain when Harry emailed over some login details. I clicked the link and found myself in the middle of a database that only a true acolyte of the Dewey decimal system could love. I had arrived at the Art Library, a digital catalog of the more than seven thousand art books Harry owned.

Seven thousand books seemed like an extraordinary number to me. How could there be any missing? There was a search field, so I typed "Hockney"; sixty-seven titles were returned.

I did the same for the other two artists and soon knew the books that were in the library. Great sleuthing, Nancy Drew. What I didn't have a clue about was how to find out which books were missing.

I had hit a brick wall in my detective work and I did what every good intern should do but usually doesn't: I asked. Back as a twenty-year-old intern, my pride or desire to please would have stopped me from pestering my boss with what I thought was a dumb question. I would have spent a few hours panicking only to produce something that wasn't right at all. But now that I was older and wiser and aware that there was no such thing as a dumb question (except "Does my butt look big in this?"), I asked Harry, who responded immediately: *Talk to Thomas Heneage. They can help.*

One speedy Google search later I knew that Thomas Heneage was not only a person but also a shop of the same name, the keeper of the books. Dressed in my new, clean black turtleneck, I popped my laptop into my bag and sped across town to Mayfair. I stood on the corner of Duke Street, studying a storefront with a set of arched windows and a display of books showcasing Caravaggio and Monet neatly stacked. There were no customers inside, only shelf after shelf of books and an intimidating set of women, deeply concentrating at their desks. I took a deep breath: I can do this. It's just a bookstore.

As I opened the door, a little bell rang, but no one came to greet me. It was not like any bookstore I had seen before. It was small, first of all, and every single square inch of shelf space was stuffed. I'm sure they must have been in some order, but I couldn't figure it out. Renaissance tomes were next to a Warhol lithograph and a biography of Artemisia Gentileschi. I wasn't sure how anyone would be able to find anything in there at all.

I waited by the front door, shifting from foot to foot nervously for about a minute. Still no one came. Finally, in a quiet voice I said, "Hello?" Out walked a woman, Elodie, who looked very smart in glasses that looked pretty real and a black turtleneck. "Can I help you?" she asked.

"Good afternoon," I began in my most enthusiastic and polite voice, rehearsing what I had practiced on the ride over. "I'm helping Harry Blain add to his Art Library and he'd like to know if you have any new titles for a few artists."

"Yes, of course," she replied. "Who are you looking for?"

I had written out the three artists' names on a paper that I handed to her, still unsure of how to pronounce Ruscha.

"Yes, very good. Let's start with Hockney. Yes, he has a catalogue Raisinet from 1996, I'm sure you have that one already. Do you know?" she asked in a strong French accent.

"I'm sorry, the what?"

"The catalogue Raisinet."

"Hold on just one moment," I replied, flustered. "Let me have a look."

I pulled my laptop out of my bag to open up Harry's library, which seemed like the thing I was supposed to do. But in my head I was thinking: WTF is a Raisinet? Unlike Diebenkorn, I actually knew Raisinets were a movie snack (a disgusting one; stop trying so hard, raisins).

I furiously typed "Raisinets" into Google. Adorable but irrelevant images of the California Raisins kept popping up as the woman continued talking about the Raisinets. "Ruscha has two newish ones, of paintings and printed materials," she said. "What about Richter's from 2010? Do you have that catalogue Raisinet?"

She kept repeating the phrase over and over, but it didn't make any more sense than the first time she had said it. I was stumped again, twice in one day, but this time, I couldn't overcome my pride.

Finally, I tried searching "catalogue" "Raisinet," and "art." Honestly, what did people do before Google? Within the first ten search items returned was the phrase I had been looking for: "catalogue raisonné." It is not, in fact, a chocolate-covered raisin but a comprehensive reference work that listed all works of art by an artist.

I learned later that, in a world where books are important, a catalogue raisonné is the most important. It's the encyclopedia of every piece of work an artist has ever created, the reference point in any sale to show that a work was definitively made by a particular artist, the proof of provenance. "In this world, information is everything," Harry told me once. "Basically, if it's not in the catalogue raisonné, it doesn't exist."

Over time, some catalogues raisonnés had become, themselves, incredibly valuable, some going for tens of thousands. I started to see how Harry's seven-thousand-book library was not just useful for the works he was selling but probably worth a lot in and of itself, and I understood why Thomas Heneage was such an important stakeholder—it controlled access to the books.

Elodie and I browsed through the catalogues raisonnés to determine which ones Harry was missing and she told me to leave the list with her. I said goodbye and walked out the door with the bell tinkling behind me. I was both proud that I had managed my first task and mortified that it had been such a close call. Clearly, I should have spent less time shopping for yoga/dress pants and more time learning French.

Other younger, fresh-out-of-grad-school art interns might not have had as much life experience as I did ("You're not old, Mommy, you're seasoned," Theo regularly says), but they knew a lot more about art than me. I foolishly assumed that I would have retained plenty of knowledge from my degree days, even though they were more than fifteen years behind me. But I remembered very little and was way out of my league; it wasn't just the imposter syndrome talking.

Deep breath. It was only day one. When I got home, I ordered two books with overnight delivery about selling contemporary art. I spent the rest of the afternoon creating a comprehensive list of the Art Library's missing books for the three artists Harry had requested. At the end of the day, I was rewarding myself with a bag of mini Reese's Pieces for a job well done (a far superior snack than Raisinets), when my phone buzzed.

Nice work on the books, Harry's message said. *Come by the house tomorrow, I have a few pieces I want you to see.*

With my head swimming with new knowledge, I made my way to Harry's the next morning on what was a truly gorgeous day. It had been so long since I had left the house for work, and with the sun shining, I was actually giddy. Commuting, normally among my least favorite of activities, was a novelty after so long cooped up inside. Even though lockdown was officially over, there were few cars on the road and none of the usual traffic. I zipped down the northern border of Hyde Park, and through the trees I saw that the sidewalks were full of bike riders and pedestrians vying for space; everyone had come out to experience what could be the last vestiges of summer. Londoners were great at taking advantage of nice weather because one never knew when it might be the last time they saw the sun for weeks.

I had come to Harry's prepared to greet the dreaded Rebel face-to-face. I had a pocket full of doggie treats to surreptitiously sneak her, once again relying on food as my go-to "please like me" move. I rang the bell to the sound of her barking, but this time when she greeted me she quieted down quickly as I slipped her a snack. She still jumped all over me but had not yet tried to take a bite out of my skin. Progress.

Harry looked casual but cool in his jeans, checked blazer, and white shirt. He was having a good week. "I sold two Banksys and an Ai Weiwei," he told me, coffee in hand. He had already met a client for breakfast that morning, someone who wanted to show him a Lucian Freud painting that they might want to sell. In all of his years in the business, Harry could hazard a fair guess of how much a painting might be worth on sight, but this process was still elusive to me.

"How do you do it?" I asked him. "Figure out how much a painting is worth?" In a world where books go for tens of thousands, and values can double or triple in a matter of weeks, where did one even start?

"I'll do better than tell you," he said. "I'll show you."

We walked into his living room. One wall was filled with art books (not all seven thousand but a few hundred of his favorites). Across from the books was a piece so new, the bottom half of it was still wrapped in bubble wrap.

He unwrapped it to reveal four panels of a bright canvas, an abstract portrait by David Hockney, one of the darlings of British contemporary art. The image was of a man—Hockney's devoted, longtime assistant, David Graves—who had died the year before.

"I just bought this," Harry said, showing me on his phone how the full image looked when put together. It was huge, and towered over him even though he was more than six feet tall. Although Hockney was known for his portraits, this one had been out of the public eye for years, not having been exhibited since 1983.

"How much do you think this is worth?" Harry asked me.

I had absolutely no idea. I knew from my research the day before that the price of a Hockney had skyrocketed in recent years; in 2018, one of his swimming pool paintings sold at auction for $90 million.

"Seven figures?" I guessed.

"Definitely," Harry replied. "But how much?"

I shrugged. "Beats me."

Lots of factors go into pricing a work, he explained, but you have to start with research. Where had it been exhibited? Who had owned it? Being able to track where something had been seen was part of why having an extensive art book collection mattered so much.

Then you had to figure out, if you could, how much it had previously sold for. This was not straightforward; auction prices were available using the Artnet database, but private sales, where the bulk of the big-money deals happen, weren't available publicly. Harry left me with the homework of trying to accurately price the Hockney. Even if it was in the tens of millions, most of his clients wouldn't balk. They were super-collectors, at the top tier of the market. These were people who would take you in their private jet to three different countries in one day to visit artists' studios and buy things on the spot. A price like $90 million might incite a raised eyebrow, but for some, that was only a fraction of their total art budget. "These are people who don't need more houses or yachts or planes," Harry said.

"Surely you only need one plane?" I said.

"Well, you never know," he replied, explaining that, maybe, you might need a big one or a small one, depending on how many passengers you wanted to carry or how long the landing strip was on your private island. There was a true story I heard about a collector who was building up his collection from scratch. To do so, he was spending about $100 million on art. Every month. For two years.

At that level of largesse, there was only so far research would get you. It might put you in the ballpark, but only a seasoned professional could decide where to aim their bat. Gut, experience, and what we in Miami would call *cojones* were all part of the formula. You had to have some big ones to look someone in the eye and tell them you wanted to sell them artfully arranged splotches of oil paint on a square canvas for $90 million.

On my way home that day, I decided to stop by the Tate Modern. I felt like I needed some time to transition between contemplating multimillion-dollar works of art and discussing homework and dinner and laundry. Plus, I was in the mood to see, in real life, a few of the works by Hockney, Richter, and Ruscha that I had come across during my book search.

In spite of my disastrous meeting with Nigel, that junior curator, back in 2003, I had always loved spending time at the Tate Modern. In London I lived only a short walk away and had a family membership. I made a point of bringing my twins on a regular basis, exposing them to art at an early age so they know their Ofili from their *Ophelia*. I was conscious that I never wanted them to feel like they needed fake glasses to fit in. Even if most of what they did was giggle about all the boobies.

The Tate boasted a whole set of rooms devoted to Ed Ruscha, so I started there. I wandered around the exhibition chuckling to myself a lot. Ruscha's work was whimsical and thought-provoking. He superimposed text over images ("Pay

Nothing Until April") and loved words, having started his working life in advertising before becoming a full-time artist. I felt a particular affinity for people who had switched careers, for obvious reasons.

In a small corner of the exhibition, there was a lone business card. Apparently, no one could pronounce his name ever, so he had some printed that said:

EDWARD RUSCHA
(ED-WERD REW-SHAY)
YOUNG ARTIST

I guess I wasn't the only one who needed some guidance. Maybe everyone in the art world had a little bit of imposter syndrome. Just like me, they were figuring it out as they went along.

Chapter 11
Mabel and Me, Best of Friends

The days turned into weeks, and I was well into my time with Harry as the leaves were beginning to fall. I had spent the morning gallery-hopping around Mayfair—competitive research, of course—when Harry messaged to see if I could pop over to Sotheby's to pick up a piece for him. His text said that it was a work by Adam McEwen that hadn't sold at auction. He could have picked it up himself, but he thought perhaps I'd like the chance to see the famed auction house from the inside.

Even older than Christie's, Sotheby's was founded in 1744. It presided over prime New Bond Street real estate, sandwiched comfortably between Chloé and Fendi, its navy blue flag with gold lettering beckoning the anointed into its hallowed halls.

I had been ramping up my efforts to cultivate a sense of belonging in the art world. After #RaisinetGate2020, I had studied up, done my reading, and paid attention. I even accurately priced a painting the day before. No one was going to hand me a free pass out of feeling like a fraud, I realized, so if I wanted to consider the art world as a serious prospect, I needed to push myself. Or, at least, I needed to adopt the consultant's motto: fake it till you make it.

I entered Sotheby's, the sound of my steps echoing down a long hallway with high ceilings above me and elegant columns on either side. A security guard in a suit stopped me a few paces in. "I'm here to collect a piece for my boss," I told him through my mask.

"Of course, miss. Is it a painting?" he asked.

I had absolutely no idea—Harry had not told me much. "Probably. I mean maybe. Yes."

"Paintings collection is down the corridor, miss, to the left and down the stairs."

I loved him because he called me "miss," a far superior greeting than the dreaded "ma'am." Following his directions, I passed the Sotheby's café on my left. It was midafternoon and there was an assortment of mostly older ladies and gentlemen, impeccably dressed, with towering platters of afternoon tea stacked in front of them. My eyes were drawn to an older woman in Dior, with a pristine blond bob and enormous sunglasses, cucumber sandwich in hand. She took a delicate bite, so as not to smudge her lipstick, as she sat with three men in suits who were all paying her rapt attention. She was clearly a Sotheby's regular, someone who belonged there, I thought to myself, as I followed the signs to the collections counter.

Collecting a painting at Sotheby's required passing through several gates, figuratively speaking: I had to show my ID first and would be given a token to take to another room, where someone would retrieve the work for me, check my ID again, and send me on my way. Even waiting in line for my token sent an electric current up my spine. I had a reason to be there. Yes, I was basically a glorified courier, but it felt like a step in the right direction. This was a place I wanted to open its doors to me.

After my ID was checked, I was handed the elusive token and given directions to the collections gallery for my pickup. Up the stairs, down the stairs, turn right. After getting lost twice, I made my way to a plain, nondescript-looking room with a counter. No glitz or glamour, just a place that looked a lot like the layaway counter at the mall, manned by a burly gentleman.

I handed him my token and ID again, and he disappeared into a back room, returning five minutes later with a round panel that he was holding more delicately than I would have assumed possible given how big his hands were. The work was titled *Untitled* and the Sotheby's-headed paper that came along with it told me it was from 2012, graphite mounted on aluminum, about forty inches in diameter and priced at fifteen thousand pounds. It had somber black and gray rectangular slashes across it. Not that it mattered, but I personally didn't like it and could see why it had failed to sell at auction.

"Can you confirm this is the correct item?" he asked, gruffly.

Hmm. I had no idea. I didn't know beforehand what I was supposed to be picking up. "Umm, I think so? Let me just see," I said, not entirely sure how I was in fact going to see. Google, my usual savior? Not sure I could put in "Untitled" and expect something useful to come up.

Then I remembered. The week before, at Harry's house, he showed me a work that was about to be shipped to a client. But he didn't want to show me the front. We flipped the painting over and looked at the back panel, plain wood covered in stickers. Galleries put labels on the back of works they had sold in order to identify some key facts about them—artist, year painted, catalogue raisonné number—as well as to mark their territory. It was a far more enlightened method than how dogs did it but was still surprisingly analog. A work that had changed hands a lot might have multiple sticky labels on the back, its journey from one buyer to another told in Avery 94200s. "You often learn more about a painting by looking at the back than the front," Harry had said.

I picked up the panel with confidence, looking for a label or simply hoping something might come to me through osmosis. But as I turned the work over to see the back, my hand faltered and it slipped.

The next seconds played in my head in slow motion: *Untitled* fell off the counter, crashing to the ground, cracking in half. I made a fool of myself in Sotheby's and would never be allowed back in. Harry would be furious. I would be forced to sell one child, or possibly both depending on the going rate, to make back the fifteen thousand pounds.

But, thankfully, my knight in shining Sotheby's polo shirt slid his hands underneath mine, catching *Untitled* before it had slipped more than two inches. "Why don't I just wrap this for you?" he said slowly. "And put it in a bag."

He went into the back and I used the respite to slow my hyperventilating breath. After an extra-long time—I'm sure to triple-wrap the work to keep it safe from me—he returned with the piece swaddled and deposited in a tote bag. My breathing had slowed and I was calm. "Thank you so much," I told him.

"Anytime, butterfingers," he replied, winking.

I retraced my steps out the door, this time with that coveted blue Sotheby's bag in my hand. As I sauntered down the hall, the old lady with the dark glasses nodded at me, respectfully. I nodded back, with a small smile.

Little by little I had been trying to whittle away at my insecurity about my lack of art credentials. Unlike Broadway, which felt like a fairy tale instead of a job, and fitness, which was physically exhausting and intellectually too similar to the business career I was trying to leave, the art world in contrast was starting to seem like it was, or could one day be, part of my real life. The internship itself had been going really well; I had not (yet) made any multimillion-pound mistakes, and even Rebel was starting to like me.

There was another addition to my arsenal too; a few days earlier I had been introduced to Mabel. She wasn't a blue-haired secretary with a gravelly voice and a cigarette hanging out of her mouth, like the name suggested, or a friendly gallery assistant. (Do those exist?) She was a database, a thing of beauty. In a world where knowledge was power, Mabel was the secret weapon.

I had been surprised to find out that across the art industry, even at the highest levels, knowledge about pricing paintings was sparsely distributed, piecemeal, and fragmented. The sums of money that Harry and his colleagues dealt with were so extraordinary, I would have expected there was a much more systematized way of knowing the price history of a work in order to justify the eye-watering amounts one would be expected to pay for it next. But in most cases, it was the equivalent of fake glasses: false confidence, the emperor naked on the throne telling Baron So-and-So that yes, this lobster telephone was worth $180 million.

Mabel was the antidote to that, a veritable treasure trove of neat categories and well-ordered records. If you needed to know the last time someone offered you a big Damien Hirst and for how much, Mabel knew whether it had sold or not. The proper way to address an invitation to Lady von Shnicklefritz (and also which of her ex-husbands is she or is she not estranged from)? Ask Mabel. A client requested one of Warhol's *Mao*s, and a quick search on Mabel pulled up thirty-six of them.

I loved having Mabel in my life. In a world I had found to be spontaneous and driven by passion, without a logical foothold to park my left brain in, Mabel was a refreshing dose of order amid the chaos. She gave me a sense of control over a highly uncontrollable world. Whether that control was real or imagined, it almost didn't matter. I needed it badly.

Around me, there was a strange aura of normalcy in this weird period we would come to know as the valley between two horrendous pandemic peaks. In some ways, things felt routine. Theo and Lola were back in school and we had left the sheep and the ice and the rural safety of Skye for busy London once more. The country was no longer in lockdown, so every day I had somewhere to go and something to do. I wore real clothes most days (okay, some days). Life, after being unrecognizable for so long, was starting to feel strangely . . . normal.

I had been desperately waiting for normalcy to return. Over lockdown I had made bullet-point list after bullet-point list of things I was going to do when restrictions were lifted. (Eighty-five percent of them were food-related: Eat tacos. Eat dumplings. Eat literally anything not made by my own hands.) After so many months of abnormality, feeling normal was good—right?

But my life in the art world wasn't really my normal life. Like a patina that could be rubbed away with a vigorous scrub, it was a break from reality, a vacation from normal, not normal itself. Normal was my old job, my old patterns, and my old life. Falling back into it would have been the path of least resistance; I could easily let the current of routine wash over me and pull me back under.

At the beginning of my internship journey, I had told

everyone I was just taking a little time away, going on sabbatical, which always implied that I would return. It was my backup plan—if a new career didn't materialize, maybe instead I would just realize in the process of doing the internships that I already had everything I needed to be happy. But even contemplating the idea of going "back to normal" incited a cold sweat. I didn't want my old normal. I didn't want to go back to sitting behind a desk and staring at a computer screen with an inbox of hundreds of emails, fixing the margins on slide deck after slide deck or reconciling expenses or creating proposals for new work. I wanted to be creative, challenged, pushed. I wanted to do something different. I didn't even know if normal still existed—but whether it did or not, a stubborn part of me was sure that my past wasn't where my future lay.

One thing I was sure of, if nothing else, was that I needed to use my time with Harry as an opportunity to see and experience as much of the art world as I could. Before diving into my "market research," I had never realized most of London's 1,500 contemporary art galleries are actually open to the public and free to enter. I had always assumed that, if I wasn't going to buy anything, I wouldn't be welcome. I'm not sure galleries go out of their way to disabuse people of that notion—they are imposing spaces for the uninitiated—but, the fact was, I was spoiled for choice when it came to finding free exhibitions of new, hip, and usually super-weird contemporary art to experience.

Pandemic precautions had made prebooking essential, so I planned my viewing schedule in advance. One week on my designated "gallery day," I went to the White Cube in London's Bermondsey neighborhood to catch an exhibition called *Chicxulub* by a Vietnamese Danish artist named Danh Vo. We were in the midst of a September heat wave. There is usually just one brief week each year when London temperatures rise to anything one could call "hot," and this was it. It was sweltering, and a city where air conditioners are seen as the height of wasteful luxury did not cope well with temperature extremes. Frankly, neither did I.

It was stifling under my mask. I noted that, as I waited outside for my entry time, the White Cube's usually glass-fronted entrance was covered with cardboard and tape. *Huh*, I thought, *they must be constructing something*, not realizing that this unusual feature, like many others, was actually part of the exhibition. Not knowing what's supposed to be "the art" and what's not happened to me a lot in contemporary exhibitions (and, I suspect, not just to me).

I pushed through the cardboard doors and entered the foyer. I felt the fires before I saw them: wood-burning stoves, to be precise, set up all around the gallery. The fires were burning furiously while people dressed in black—staff? performance artists? stokers?—continually fed the stoves with more wood. I don't think Vo could have necessarily predicted the heat wave, but the effect was like I was wearing a parka. In a sauna. In hell. In the corner, there was a fire extinguisher and I questioned whether that was part of the exhibition or the fire code. I never found out.

I loved that exhibition, and so many of the others I saw during my internship, but I certainly couldn't tell you why. With time, research, and a whole lot of BS, I could make something up, but the truth is that all that clever analysis wasn't really the point. Even though contemporary art is empirically so strange and interesting and often doesn't make sense (even to someone who had studied it and interned in it), it had always succeeded in making me feel *something*. The best works evoked a visceral reaction. I had been on a veritable roller coaster of emotions. I felt elated. Uncomfortable. Privileged. Out of place. Excited. Very, very hot.

Not for the first time since my internships began I felt both grateful, that I could still feel this type of passion stirring within me, and dismayed, that it seemed it had been so long since I had felt anything like that at all. After a particularly thought-provoking day spent combing through Mabel while placating Rebel, I decided to bike home from Harry's house through Hyde Park. The heat wave had passed, but the sunshine was still present, and it was too nice a day to get into a taxi or onto the Tube.

I pedaled down the park's long avenues, slowly swerving to avoid the many pedestrians, scooters, and other bikes all doing the same thing I was: taking advantage of the sunshine. In a scene that would not have been out of place in a Seurat painting, the swans were gliding across the Round Pond, diving their graceful heads under to catch stale bread thrown throughout the day by Kensington children and their nannies. A group of coworkers had opened a bottle of wine and were sharing it, albeit at a safe distance, like a modern, COVID-friendly version of Manet's *Le Déjeuner sur l'herbe*.

Over the past few weeks, I had started noticing art everywhere. A man skateboarded next to me listening to music on a radio hanging from his neck. Wasn't that a form of performance art in its own way? An advertisement had been ripped off the side of a London bus, leaving a sparse black-and-gray background, not so different from *Untitled*, the Adam McEwen I had almost dropped at Sotheby's.

I felt something being rekindled within me, a small flame that once was there, that I thought had been snuffed out when

I wasn't looking. But maybe, just maybe, it had been glowing softly, like a pilot light, waiting for a spark to set it aflame once again. I wasn't yet sure that the art world was the place for me, or if, in fact, there was a place for me in the art world. But on that gorgeous day with the sun on my skin, breeze streaming in my face, legs pumping away as I rode through the park, happy to be outside and healthy and alive, I secretly hoped that, if there was, I could find it. And that if I found it, I wouldn't have to fake it till I could make it. I'd just belong.

Chapter 12
The Course Correction

Though never a morning person, I can admit, begrudgingly, that it is reliably the best time of day to think. It was just after eight on Thursday morning in the final week of my internship with Harry, and I was sitting in my living room, the whole house around me peaceful. The sky was an unusual blue, the sun mercifully shining. A large tree hung over the sidewalk in front of our house, and I watched from the window as a squirrel shook its branches, heavy with horse chestnuts, willing them to fall. Despite the sunshine, there was a definite chill in the air. Autumn had arrived.

Though it's a season associated with the end of summer, fall to me always signified beginnings: the beginning of the school year, the beginning of a new TV season. My art internship had flown by. All three of my internships had flown by. It had been just over a year from the day I considered the beginning of my journey, the day I first blocked off my work calendar in preparation to find my first internship in a world that seemed unrecognizable from the one I was currently residing in. And it had been already more than six months since my brief, dreamlike stint in New York.

Over the past four weeks, my work with Harry had been a brilliant respite from everything happening in the world outside. There was a palpable buzzing in my brain, the good kind. *We need these books on Frankenthaler. Let's look for gallery spaces in Mayfair for our new office. Can you add this $60 million Jackson Pollock to Mabel?* The pace was quick and I loved chasing down each thread until it reached a satisfying conclusion.

It was a good distraction from the other current that would rear its ugly head sometimes in quiet moments: anxiety about the present, worry about the future, wonder at what was going to come next. Before we left Skye months earlier, I had lined up my next internship at a boutique hotel and restaurant on the island. Hospitality as an industry had always intrigued me. I loved few things more than eating a nice meal or staying at a beautiful hotel and had always wondered if I'd like being behind the front desk as much as I did being in front of it. Scotland was full of magical places, including Kinloch Lodge, where I had secured my internship. I had already started packing my suitcase and planned to head up to Skye, alone, for a couple of weeks.

"Where are you going now, Columbus?" said Carlos. He was joking, but his underlying point was clear: I was exploring again, but eventually it was going to be time to hop off the ship and commit to whatever my new world was going to be.

My last week in London, Harry and I met to check out a private sale exhibition at Christie's, *The Leaping Light*, that featured a few Hockneys Harry wanted me to see, like a piece I had been researching recently, *Still Life with TV*. Mabel's records showed that a few years ago it was being offered for around $650,000; in this sale, it was rumored to be going for $11 million to $12 million.

Walking into Christie's with Harry was like what it might have been like to wander into a high school cheerleading competition with one of the boys from NSYNC (JC, the best one, indisputably). Heads turned and everyone knew who he was and looked delighted to see him (at least to his face).

He introduced me to a few of them as "my overqualified intern." One of the hands I shook belonged to the Christie's deputy chairman of the Post-War and Contemporary Art Division. It was not lost on me that, had I actually done my internship at Christie's in that very building, that man would have been my boss's boss's boss's boss, with probably another few bosses thrown in between for good measure. Being with Harry, I had leapfrogged the hierarchy entirely.

The exhibition was beautiful and the Hockneys were particularly breathtaking. After duly making the rounds to see everything there, Harry whispering to me under his breath how much he thought each piece would sell for, we stepped outside and said our farewells. I mused how poetic it was to be nearing the official end of my internship back in the building where another version of myself, one that didn't have her Christie's internship canceled, might have been.

"Well, Christie's loss was my gain," he said. "What are you doing tomorrow? Can you come 'round the house in the afternoon? I have something I want to discuss with you," he said cryptically as we went our separate ways.

The next day, I got up early. I was meeting Harry at his house at one, nervous because I didn't know what the meeting was about, and I was worried that I had screwed something up or, worse (much worse), somehow inadvertently broken Mabel. To kill time, I decided to catch one final exhibition before leaving my official time in the art world behind—Georg Baselitz's *Darkness Goldness* at the White Cube's Mason's Yard gallery. Baselitz, a German-born artist, is best known for his paintings and sculptures of gargantuan, sort of freakishly shaped hands and feet, towering fifteen or twenty feet high.

I was completely alone in the gallery for the first few minutes. I wandered around, lost in my own thoughts, until one of the gallery staff walked in with a potential buyer. She started explaining the works to her client, clearly in sales mode, and sharing some fascinating gems of knowledge about the artist and his process. I inched closer so I could listen in.

"Baselitz uses something called a monotype printing process," she said. "First, he quickly paints an image of a hand on one canvas. Then he places a second canvas on top, presses it down, and peels it off. The first canvas gets discarded, and then he uses the second to create what will eventually become the final work."

The buyer nodded, stroking her chin in a thinking pose, and asked about the price. A six-figure amount was exchanged. Old Alisha might have gasped at that point. It was way more than I had ever spent on a piece of art myself, but I didn't even blink; I had gotten used to much bigger numbers over the last month. The buyer made some positive noises and then said how much she loved the seemingly haphazard process of making the works. The gallery employee agreed. Baselitz never knew how a work would turn out when he quickly painted each hand on the first canvas. The finished product wasn't something he had predicted, and yet he filled a gallery with them (and sold them for quite a lot of money).

"He's opening himself up to chance," she said. "He's creating happy accidents."

I left, my brain cogs whirring as I went to meet Harry at his house. "Happy accidents" was just another way to look at where I was now, not to mention it offered a much more positive spin on the idea that lots of things happened without our control.

Harry greeted me at the gate to his house, arms full of puppy paraphernalia—leash, treats, poop bags. "Do you mind if we take Rebel around the block and grab a coffee?" he asked. "We're working with her trainer on socializing her with more people. She needs to spend time with them on neutral territory first, not her own territory."

Rebel growled a little, but didn't bark at me at all, and gratefully licked my outstretched hand when I handed over my secret biscuit. It seemed like her trainer/doggie therapist's advice was working. Or maybe my constant bribery had finally won her over.

Harry, Rebel, and I walked down the block to the kind of coffee shop you might find only in the bougiest parts of major cities—one that doubled as a yoga studio and vegan restaurant. Harry went inside to order, while Rebel and I grabbed a table out front. Next to me was a frazzled-looking young woman pushing two sleeping infants in a double stroller.

"It gets better," I told her. "I promise. My twins are almost nine and I've survived this far. I even put clothes on this morning."

She looked like she couldn't decide whether to hug me or break down in tears. I remembered that feeling of complete physical and emotional exhaustion well. The idea that I would one day be able to go to the bathroom alone, much less have the headspace to do a series of internships in my dream jobs, would have seemed laughable to me then. But my own double stroller days were very far away from where I was now: nervously sitting in West London, waiting for a coffee that would have in it either milk or kale, or both.

Harry came out with my mercifully nonvegan coffee and his green flaxseed smoothie, and we caught up on the busy week. I was anxious and finding it hard to stop blathering about nothing. Once we had exhausted all polite conversation (the weather, the status of our respective children, Maria's upcoming due date, the art I had seen recently, and the latest auction house gossip), Harry paused, then said, "You know, I make a life change every five years."

He proceeded to tell me how he had started his professional career in finance and had a knack for sales. When one of his coworkers said he was leaving to start a career in the art world, he wanted Harry to join him. His own happy accident.

"I told him I didn't know anything about art," he went on, "but he said it didn't matter." They were looking for people who could sell any asset, and Harry was great at that. The art world welcomed him in, and eventually he embarked on his own journey: a series of galleries, successes and failures. I admired his resilience, and I told him as much.

"You've done it," I told him. "The thing I'm trying to do. Pivoted, picked yourself up, dusted yourself off, and done something different."

"I know, and I admire that in you," he said. "That's why I'd like to continue working together."

I was flabbergasted, to say the least. He had dropped a hint or two over the past few weeks to that effect—when I got my Blain Art email address, he was the first one to send me a note, which just said, *Welcome officially to your new career as an emerging art world star!*—but I honestly thought he was just being polite. I knew I had been doing a fairly good job, but I had been having so much fun that I had not really considered that someone would ever pay me for it.

"I've loved working with you the past few weeks," I said. "What sort of thing would you have in mind?"

"Well, what would you *like* to do?" he asked.

I thought for a moment. "I'm not really sure. I certainly wouldn't want to be dead weight. Of course, I'd want to be helpful; but I recognize that in spite of my advanced age, I'm probably not even as qualified as some recent graduate you could just hire off the street. I've loved what I've been doing, especially the research aspect of it, and I feel like I'm starting to get a hang of the commercial elements. I'm not really sure. I'm babbling," I babbled.

After a few deep breaths, I collected myself and tried again. "Maybe I could be a sort of part-time junior adviser, one or two days a week? It would depend on what you needed. And if you could afford me," I added jokingly, worried I was selling myself too short at a cut-rate price.

"How about this?" he volleyed back. "You join me as a director. We'll try just a year to start, full-time. We could discuss numbers, but you could consider a base salary plus commission. Think of how much we sell works of art for. It could be very lucrative for you."

This was not a low-risk, no-commitment offer. It was a full-on new career. I had thought maybe I could take on an assistant-type role, but a director? I was shocked, truly. Sure, I had only just learned what a catalogue raisonné was and could finally pronounce "Ruscha," but just the day before, Harry had said something about an impasto and I excused myself to go to the bathroom so I could Google it. I may have been overqualified as an intern, but I felt woefully underqualified to be a director.

"I'm flattered," I said. "I mean, really flattered. Can I ask, and I'm not trying to be funny, but why me? I know I've been helpful, at least I've tried to be. But a director? I don't have any experience besides a month as your intern."

"You're one of the smartest people I know. And more than that, you're trustworthy and people like you. Those are the two most important things in this business. The art you can learn about."

I sat there, mouth gaping.

"You don't have to answer right now," Harry said. "Think about it."

Was this really happening? The life I had thought about since 2003—a job in the art world—was being laid at my feet. I couldn't actually believe that this crazy internship idea had netted me an actual job offer. My almost-life was tantalizingly close to becoming my real life. Now that the door was open, could I do it? Did I even still want to?

I regained my composure and thanked him for his faith in me. We walked back to the house with Rebel, who looked me straight in the eye as I held both drinks and all her accessories while Harry bent down on the sidewalk outside their house to clean up her poop. I hugged Harry (once the poop had been disposed of) with gratitude.

"Thank you, again. I really would love to work something out," I said, as I turned to walk toward home. "Let me think about it? You can too, in case you change your mind. I'll be in Scotland for the next month. Why don't we talk when I return?"

He agreed and said goodbye, leaving the beautifully wrapped gift he had handed me in my care.

To clear my head, I decided to walk home, going the long way across town. I had, of course, from time to time, dreamed that one of my internship bosses would magically see potential in me and offer me a real job, but I always thought it would be just that: a dream. Getting people to agree to hire me for free had been hard enough; asking for a paycheck seemed like a bridge too far.

I called Carlos. "I don't know," I said. "How would it even work? Would I have a boss? Would I have to completely transition out of my current job? Did I have enough black turtlenecks now or would I need to buy more?"

He laughed. "Well, you have time to think about it. And to go shopping. We can discuss further when you get home. But I think you should do it. This is what you wanted, right? By the way, what's for dinner?"

I mumbled something about lasagna and hung up the phone. Yes, I was excited, and I was nervous. My art world foray had increasingly felt like one of Baselitz's happy accidents. Maybe I had actually gone down the right path after all way back in 2003; without that life-changing conversation at the Tate, I wouldn't have ended up where I found myself, with a job offer at my fingertips. If I had worked at the Tate as a postgraduate, maybe I would have ended up as disillusioned as Nigel. Maybe, instead of walking around that museum each day in awe of everything I saw, I'd be bored, tired, and traumatizing a future generation of art historians with my frustrated tirades.

Nothing about this project had gone the way I had planned, but maybe it was going to work out better than I could ever have imagined. Maybe my move into art wasn't a detour but a course correction.

Drowning out these considerations, however, was a much louder emotion: fear. That old, familiar tightness in my chest. I was scared. The idea that I could make a major career pivot into an entirely brand-new field—not just any field but one I had always dreamed of working in—was something I didn't even dare speak out loud when I was diligently laying the foundations for what I thought would be a fun year of mini-sabbaticals. Sure, I had let my mind wander now and then to the possibility that perhaps one of these internships might lead to a real job. But a senior job with a big title and an attractive salary? Even I didn't dream that big.

I had, at my fingertips, the beginnings of the new life I wanted in my grasp. If I reached just a bit farther, I could grab it.

I hated to admit this, even to myself, but I was afraid of taking such a big leap into something so new. Leaving my job, my company, my track record of achievements, my reputation as an expert, behind for something that might work out but maybe wouldn't seemed enormously risky. When doing my internships, I always had a bungee cord attached to me; I could always go back to my old job and my old life. I might not have been happy, but I was safe, the path was clear, and the cord wasn't going to snap. If I leapt into the unknown, with nothing to pull me back to safety, I didn't know what would happen. Maybe it would be better. But what if it wasn't? Why rock the boat, in the middle of a pandemic, no less? I'd had my fun—shouldn't I just return to my normal life?

The problem was that the idea of going back to "normal," whatever that was, seemed increasingly unlikely. First of all, COVID was still raging and there wasn't an end in sight. But it was more than that. I remembered a snippet of a conversation I had with my friend Kate on the very first day of my art internship, when I got that surprise message from Harry. I had been regaling her with stories from my New York stint and my workouts with Retroglow.

"So what's next?" she asked. "I mean, after the internships."

I told her I wasn't sure but that I hoped it would be different from what I had been doing before. She was happy for me. "It's the right thing," she said, "because—"

"Yeah, I know," I interrupted. "I'm just so ready for a change."

"It's not just that though," she said. "I was going to say that it seems like for a long time you've been doing too much.

And not—don't take this the wrong way—necessarily enjoying it. I mean, it's nice that you've been so in demand, but I'm not surprised you feel burned out."

Her insight gave me pause, but not because she was wrong. It was because I thought I had done a good job hiding it from everyone. Going back to that place where I said yes to everything without acknowledging the toll it took was the one thing I was most afraid of. Despite the objective awfulness that the pandemic had wrought, I had been happier— professionally, at least—in the past few months of internships than I had been in a long time. All of the challenges and mistakes and times when I felt dumb for not knowing anything, all of the sucking up to Carmen and contorting my body into weird positions for the latest virtual fitness trend and mispronouncing names of artists, all of it had made me feel alive.

In these jobs I was a novice absorbing everything, like the sponge my husband never manages to take out of the sink and put back in its place. Every day was unexpected and new and hard but rewarding, and I was having the time of my life. The pressure in my chest had lightened and I could feel the little bits of myself I thought I had lost returning to fill the space that had been created.

A permanent, full-time job, even one as empirically cool as the one Harry was offering, would erode the progress I had made, I worried. It would be fun for a few months, but in short order I'd be right back where I had started. I would have swapped my outfit and donned my fake glasses and my turtleneck with aplomb, but I would get into bed and wake up in the morning with the same itchy feet, the same listlessness, the sense that every day was just like the next, and there it would continue until I died. I just wanted to hold on to how I felt, right then and there, that warm internship feeling, for a little while longer.

As I arrived home, I had to put the quandary behind me. Inside were two hungry children, a tired husband, and a half-empty suitcase that was ready to be packed for the month in Scotland ahead. Three internships in and I was left with more questions than answers. I desperately hoped that a moment of enlightenment was just around the corner.

Chapter 13
The Road to Skye Is Paved with Good Intentions

Until 1995, the only way to get to the Isle of Skye was by boat. Large ferries, built to shepherd vehicles and passengers (human, ovine), crossed the sea several times a day from the northwest coast of Scotland. Their sturdy frames could withstand rolling waves that brought nausea to even those with the stoutest of sea legs; their oxidized exteriors were designed to take wild sprays of rain and hail and wind to safely deliver tourists and locals and farmers and builders and anyone who wanted a taste of the Misty Isle. Except when the boat was canceled due to inclement weather. Which happened a lot.

The weather in Skye is, first and foremost, wet. It rains about 230 days per year, and its average temperature is a balmy 51°F. But if you're hardy enough to withstand the weather—and the midges, a unique breed of bloodsucking insects whose swarming tendencies put Miami's famous mosquitos to shame—Skye is one of the most magically beautiful places on earth. It has craggy peaks and rolling hills, rocky beaches full of hidden mysteries, rivers, and waterfalls, and no shortage of tumbledown castles where fairies once lived and ghosts still do.

Naturally, a Miami girl with a penchant for city living and impractical shoes sticks out a little amid the peat bogs and winding burns of the isle. I surprise most everyone I meet in London when I describe my other life on a tucked-away island wearing hiking boots and chilling with my closest neighbors, the sheep.

In my heart, I will always be a native Floridian; my body, having spent the largest part of its life at or below sea level, was always more accustomed to low-lying beaches and swamps than hills and mountains. Even inland, the landscapes of my youth were flat: the smooth, boggy Everglades, the long and never-ending ranchland of Central Florida. The only heights scaled for most of my adulthood were man-made and reached by elevator, usually to a rooftop bar.

"Why would you leave Miami for"—disdainful pause—"this?" strangers asked when they met me. I usually rattled off some well-rehearsed answer: that I loved the change of seasons or got bored with too much sunshine. However, the truth was that even I was a bit perplexed as to how I ended up so far from home on the rugged and rough Isle of Skye and, more than that, had come to love it.

Practically speaking, my journey began in the backseat of an Uber. I was in London, the year was 2015, I was late (again), and it was pouring rain (as usual). I was on my way to view a potential party venue for the twins' upcoming fourth birthday. Big birthday parties—where kids overate cake and took home goody bags full of candy and cheap plastic toys you could bulk-buy in packs of eighteen—were a key holdover of my Americanism, even after a decade of living in the UK. My fellow parents, British or from other parts of the globe, didn't make a big deal of kids' birthday parties. Half the time, they didn't even bother hosting one. But I was an American and, dammit, what's more American than wasting money on useless crap and an event that your children won't even remember?

That morning, while typing out a profuse apology to the party venue manager from the backseat, I was startled by a jolt to the car. Although we were stopped at a red light, a big white van had bumped into us. The van's driver, a middle-aged white Englishman with a protruding belly and a profound sense of self-righteousness, got out and started yelling racist epithets at my driver, a young recent immigrant from Pakistan. I snapped a photo of his license plate with my phone and gave the Uber driver my business card, telling him to call me if he needed a witness for an insurance claim. Then I left a big tip and got out, deciding to try my luck running in the rain. I arrived at the venue drenched and fifteen minutes late, apologizing again, before setting out to measure if a bouncy castle would fit in the room.

A month or so later, I sat in the waiting room of the Uber driver's lawyer's office. He had messaged me, asking if I could issue a brief statement about the accident. It was inconvenient, and I might normally have said no, but I knew he was innocent; plus, sticking it to the racist driver of the white van was a bonus.

As I waited for my appointment, I picked up the closest magazine, an out-of-date *Condé Nast Traveler*, and was brainlessly skimming it when I spied a small blurb about an island off the northwest coast of Scotland called Eilean Shona. Once a place frequented by *Peter Pan* author J. M. Barrie as a child, and rumored to be the real-life inspiration for Neverland, the island had been bought by Vanessa Branson (sister of Virgin Atlantic's Richard), and she had built a few lovely, rustic cottages there that were rented by the week. The island had no cars or bridges and could be accessed only by boat. Most notably, there was no Wi-Fi or cell phone service. I ripped out the page and pocketed it, just as the lawyer called me in for me to tell him no, I didn't suffer any sort of neck injuries, but yes, the driver of the van was a real asshole.

The Uber driver got his settlement, but I couldn't get the idea of Eilean Shona out of my head. No, there were no rooftop cocktails or guarantees of sunshine, but the idea of being completely disconnected from the outside world seemed too good to be true. Ever since I had gone back to work after having the twins, it seemed I was never not "on." I was usually the only parent on my executive teams at work and felt like I had to work twice as hard, lest I give the impression that people already seemed to have: mothers were lazy and not to be trusted.

I'd be doubly dedicated during working hours, then would rush home and switch to doubly perfect mom mode. Dinner, bath, bedtime, and then, once the twins were finally asleep, I transitioned into trying to be a good spouse who feigned interest and didn't just fall asleep in the middle of a story about *Star Trek*. I had reached a point where I wasn't sure if I could switch off anymore, even if I wanted to.

That October, we piled the twins and the dog onto the sleeper train for an overnight trip and, in the morning, drove three hours to the parking lot of Castle Tioram, an atmospheric ruin on the shores of Loch Moidart that overlooked our new island home for the week, Eilean Shona. We left the car there and carried two giant suitcases, about a dozen bags of groceries and supplies, matches, flashlights, all manner of candy, a bed for the dog, and everything else we thought we might need for a week of isolation and hauled it onto a small dinghy, manned by Paul, the manager of the properties. After a short, choppy jaunt across the loch in the misty rain, with mountains rising behind us and the Atlantic Ocean churning in the distance, Paul dropped us off at the pier. "See you in a week," he said cheerfully, pointing us in the direction of our cottage, a short walk away. And then we were completely alone.

What followed was a week of total relaxation. We slept, read, assembled jigsaw puzzles, and played board games. During the day, we wandered as far as the twins' tiny legs would carry them, through forests where dew hung delicately on the branches all day and night, and the only noises we heard were from birds and the breeze (and every few minutes, a child complaining that they were hungry and/or needed to pee). We cooked hearty meals, feasting on mussels we foraged from the shore outside our cottage. At night, we roasted marshmallows in the fire pit under a canopy of thousands of stars. After years of living in cities, I had almost forgotten they were there.

Most important, we were free from all of our external obligations. No one could call or email. There were no meetings to rush to, no school to get ready for. Not a tweet was sent or received. Time slowed down and the hours drifted by gently, like waves lapping on the shore. I remember feeling as if I had truly exhaled for the first time in years.

As we set foot back on the mainland, our phones pinging with missed messages, texts, and emails, I used my reactivated 4G signal to immediately book us a cabin for October of the following year. For that trip, we decided to add on one night on the nearby Isle of Skye, a place we had heard about but never been to. We found a hotel called Kinloch Lodge that was dog friendly and kid friendly and had incredible food (the holy trifecta).

That whole year long, I dreamed of Scotland and, when we returned to the Highlands, it was as if a strange and inexplicable alchemy occurred. It's not an obvious connection. There is no "Mac" in my name, no clan background, definitely no Scottish heritage in my lineage on either the Cuban or Jewish sides of my family. I had never lived in a rural place, never put on a wet suit, and didn't know what "waterproofs" were. (They are pants that are waterproof! What will they think of next?)

All I know is that when I drove over the Skye Bridge for the first time, the outline of the Cuillin mountains on my right and the expansive Loch Alsh on my left, I felt like I had found a place I wanted to be part of and to make part of me. The following year we bought our house only 3.3 miles from Kinloch Lodge, which soon became a home away from home (away from home).

The Kinloch Lodge building was designed in the 1670s as a farmhouse, then became the hunting lodge of the Macdonald clan in the eighteenth century, until it was transformed in the 1970s into a hotel and restaurant by the current Lord Macdonald, Godfrey, and his wife Claire, a well-known chef. After decades of work that turned it from dilapidated pile to destination for the savvy traveler, they passed the management down to their daughter Isabella, who still runs it today. We were instantly charmed by every detail—the special mocktails the bartender whipped up just for the twins; the managers, Jamie and Krissy, at the front desk who were able to anticipate our every need after even just a few days; the room with a claw-foot bathtub that overlooked the loch and surrounding mountains. And, dear god, the food.

Our first visit, I had met Isabella and we had stayed in touch. Isabella had the unique ability to make guests feel like they were staying in her family home. Tall, with curly blond hair and a deep voice like Bea Arthur with a light brogue, she had charmed me from our first meeting. The fact that she regularly called me her favorite guest helped.

In the early days of planning my internships, before the pandemic made planning anything seem like a foolhardy act, I already knew I wanted to work at Kinloch. True, I had not exactly dreamed of a career in hospitality as a child (except at McDonald's—didn't every kid want to wear the headset and take orders for Happy Meals over the drive-through speaker?), but I was not a kid who stayed in a lot of hotels. When my family traveled, we mostly frequented motels or places with the word "resort" or "inn" in the title, designed to distract from the fact that they were, in fact, motels. Plane tickets were outside the realm of affordability for most of my childhood, and our family vacations were always road trips. Every year my parents and brothers and I piled into my mom's gigantic Astro van, which was white with pink stripes on the side and looked like a race car that someone had inflated like a Macy's parade balloon, and drove up from Miami through Florida, Georgia, and the Carolinas.

My parents must have had some inkling of where we would sleep every night, but these were not the types of places where one needed to make reservations. On one memorable trip, we arrived close to midnight. We were shown to our rooms, the walls the standard-issue combination of murky brown and muddy green, and, as we pulled back the bedcovers, exhausted and ready to pass out, we discovered hundreds of dead roaches. We left so fast you could hear our tires screeching along the deserted stretch of I-95.

Still, I loved motels. I loved the big pools in the center, surrounded by lawn chairs, where you could always find another
kid or two interested in a game of swim tag. I loved the ice
machines down the hallway, always excited when our room
was right next door to one. I mostly just loved the thrill of
being away from home and being somewhere new. Hotels,
motels, whatever number of stars they had or didn't have,
were the gateway to adventure and excitement; a new world
that I had yet to explore; a new person I had yet to become.
The good ones all share one thing: the chance to step out of
your normal life and be whoever you want to be for a while,
no judgments.

As that was exactly what I was looking to do now, hospitality seemed like an obvious choice. I also assumed I'd be
able to eat anything I wanted at any time, which seemed like
the best possible perk that any job could ever offer. I thought
about Kinloch's food often during lockdown, daydreaming
that maybe I could just show up to the empty building and all
the plates and cups and silverware would come to life like in
Beauty and the Beast and sing to me and serve me something
delicious and I wouldn't even have to do the dishes. I had
missed hotels terribly since my teary final checkout at the Ace
in New York. Spending my days working in one felt at that
point like it would be the height of luxury.

Like working in theater and fitness and even to some
degree art, working at a hotel required a certain amount of
performance in the role that created an orchestrated ambience
for the customer. But like with those fields, here, too, I had
very little idea of what went on behind the curtain. Perhaps
one day I would even consider running a place like Kinloch somewhere myself. The biggest plus to working in any
tourist-adjacent industry is that you could do it almost

anywhere. I could run a hotel in Skye or Sydney or Singapore or anywhere I fancied, traveling the world with a purpose and a job to do (plus a paycheck). I didn't know yet if that was true. But Kinloch was the perfect place to learn.

Or at least it was until the first lockdown in 2020, when the hotel closed from March through July, some of its busiest months of the year. As soon as it finally reopened, I agonized over the appropriateness, or inappropriateness, of asking if I could intern there. I knew it had been a horrifically challenging period for the entire industry, but I also knew they were expecting a busy autumn, as UK travelers, weary from months of lockdown in the city, craved nature, fresh air, and good food.

Maybe they could use an enthusiastic, if inexperienced, pair of hands? I drafted my pitch to Isabella. Then I redrafted it. Eight times. Then it sat in my drafts folder for another week, just waiting for me to press send, but I couldn't do it.

"What are you afraid of?" Carlos asked, as my mouse hovered over the send button for the twelfth time that day.

"I'm afraid she'll say no," I said.

"Well, you won't know unless you ask."

I held my breath and clicked. The final draft was short but sweet. I explained my internship project and asked if we could have coffee so I could tell her more. I attached my résumé, as I doubted she had any idea of my actual skills, besides what she knew about me as a hotel guest: I would eat anything if it was atop a bowl of pasta, and I never made my bed.

To my absolute delight, she wrote back the next day, and we set a date to meet in August, just before I traveled to London to start my internship with Harry. The morning of, I was a nervous wreck. I had put on makeup exactly twice in the previous five months and had forgotten how to apply eyeliner.

I probably shouldn't have been nervous, but I was. I was a CEO with a track record, I knew Isabella liked me, and I had already done a few internships, so my filing skills were on point. But I was intimidated nonetheless—would it seem like I was a "Patagonia-wearing Harvard tourist," someone who could afford to stay as a guest trying to have a fun escape where others were making their living? Had I put her in a situation where she felt like she couldn't refuse me because I was a loyal customer? Or worse, would she refuse me because of that?

The twins offered to help me prepare by doing a mock interview. They sat on the sofa and peppered me with questions like "Why do you want to work at Kinloch?" and "Do you know how to make spaghetti, and can you make some right now?"

When we finished, they told me I was hired. I only hoped Isabella would be so easily swayed.

The drive from my house in Skye to Kinloch was short and sweaty. I was nervous, and as I walked in through the large wooden doors, Isabella greeted me with her patented warmth. She hugged me and I melted into that hug even though we weren't supposed to be hugging during a pandemic. Isabella is a great hugger; she goes full into it, with maximum arm wrap. Plus she always smells wonderful—vaguely floral, with woody undertones—and her scent lingers on you for an hour or two afterward.

We sat down on two green velvet armchairs by the window. I smiled.

"I'm so nervous," Isabella began.

"What? Why?" I laughed. "I'm the one who should be nervous."

"You're our most treasured guests," she told me. "What if you never come back? I don't want what happens behind the scenes to ruin the magic. I can't very well ask you to come and make beds," she said.

"Please!" I begged. "I would love you to let me make beds!" I launched into my hard sell and told her all about what I had done in my previous internships in New York and with Frankie. I told her about filling the water jug and the Super-YAYsies Instagram posts. It seemed to convince her. With only a little cajoling, she agreed that I could join her staff for a month, rotating in and out of different roles: kitchen, restaurant, bar, front of house, and office. I'd get a taste of every part of the business. And, I assumed, a lot of the food.

Just as we opened our calendars to pick a start date, an older English woman walked into the drawing room. She wore a twinset and pearls that matched her blond bob and carried a designer bag on her arm. Isabella switched into hospitality mode. "Welcome to Kinloch," she said. "Can I be of help in any way?"

"Not at all, I'm just looking around. We were here once many years ago," she responded in a southern English drawl.

"How lovely," Isabella responded. "Did you stay here?"

"Heavens no," twinset lady exclaimed. "It was much too expensive."

"Well, we like to think of ourselves as a luxury," Isabella tactfully replied, as I eyed the woman's handbag, which cost the equivalent of three months' rent in my first Manhattan apartment.

"Yes, but still," the woman said, "should luxury really be that expensive?"

I stifled a laugh, but Isabella continued to chat with the woman politely and with the utmost diplomacy. My first lesson in hospitality: the customer is always right, even when they are so very wrong.

We said goodbye, my start date firmly fixed for the first week of October. I was initially elated, but on the drive home, my excitement quickly turned to fear. What if it doesn't work out, if we go back into lockdown, if it all gets canceled again? But as I drove back to our house, mountains on all sides, I did what I always did in Scotland. I exhaled. If the past few months had taught me anything, it was that I could figure out how to deal with whatever twists and turns would be thrown my way.

A few months later, in October, I made my way back up to Skye from London, alone. Carlos and the twins would join me in two weeks. My internship was starting in two days and my shifts for the first week, in the restaurant, were on the schedule alongside everyone else's. Everything I had hoped for was actually going to happen. In spite of the pandemic conspiring to foil my carefully laid plans at every turn, I was going to manage to complete almost a year of internships.

On the stunning two-hour drive from the train station, I tried to listen to music—getting to choose a playlist was a rare treat—but my mind was busy. I had Harry's job offer hanging over my head, and after Kinloch, I had no further internships lined up. Was I going to be ready for reentry into the real world? And what about the pandemic? Cases were rising, and while no one was saying the word "lockdown" again yet, it felt like it was on the tip of everyone's tongues.

Fear expanded inside me, like air filling up a balloon, but I closed my eyes and counted to ten. Ahead of me, I had a month at Kinloch that appeared as if it wasn't going to be canceled or indefinitely postponed. Unlike on Broadway, in fitness, or even in the art world, I had a sneaking suspicion I was going to be great at the hospitality industry.

The positive side of being a people pleaser was that I was a total people person. Soon enough I'd be delighting customers with my witty repartee, pouring wine with one hand while directing tourists to the best local beaches with the other, and sneaking leftovers of Kinloch's glorious food as often as I could. I was going to slay, Miami style, and show everyone the *sazón* they had been missing in this luxury property in the wilds of Scotland.

Chapter 14
In Which I Am Terrible at Everything

It was dark outside my car—the moon bright enough to illu-minate the driveway but not much more. The engine was off, the radio and the heating off too. My keys were in my hand, my front door a mere twenty feet away. But I could not make it to that door.

The human foot has twenty-six bones, thirty joints, and more than one hundred muscles, tendons, and ligaments. Each one of these individual components was aching with pain. Which was why I had been parked outside my house for sixteen minutes now, unable to motivate myself out of the car and into my bed so I could pass out in a heap, smelling potently of roasted meat and kitchen grease.

After eight straight days of working in the Kinloch restau-rant, parts of my feet that I didn't even know could possibly hurt, hurt. The tips of my toes! The webbing between them! And they weren't the only things injured. My pride was wounded, too.

By anyone's definition, I was not a natural at hospitality. In spite of all my fitness efforts over the previous months, my nearly forty-year-old bones and joints and metatarsals, softened by years of office work, were not cut out for a life in the restaurant business. I had to shift from heel to heel all day long just to remain upright and took frequent bathroom breaks just to sit down for a few minutes without showing my coworkers—who did this every day without complaint—that I was worn out.

Ever since my first split shift of this internship, eight days earlier, I had been lagging behind and in agony. I was on the schedule for 8:00 a.m. but woke up at six thirty, before the alarm went off. I warily eyed the pitch-black "morning" sky (the sun wouldn't rise for another hour at least) and wondered if I wasn't a little bit nuts. The hotel was a six-minute drive away. I put coffee on, lighting a small fire in the fireplace to warm up the living room. A decadent treat.

Once partially caffeinated, I got dressed in head-to-toe black, as I had been instructed by Isabella over email in the days before I started. I called the kids and Carlos, who were back in London and getting ready for school. "Wish me luck on my first day," I told them. "I'm nervous."

"Don't worry, Mommy," Theo chirped. "I'm always nervous at the beginning, but then I get used to it and it starts to be really fun."

Like every other internship I had done so far, I really didn't have much of a clue what to expect. But at this moment, I wasn't focused on the actual work so much as on the eating situation. I assumed the guests would eat their breakfasts first, which usually ran until around ten, and then, once they had finished, we (as in staff, including me!) would get a crack at the leftovers. Eleven would be too late for my first meal of the day.

I needed some sustenance before heading out the door, lest I get fired on the first day for getting caught with a stolen scone.

I greased a frying pan to make a quick egg sandwich and flashed back to being alone in my noisy New York Airbnb on another "first day," seven months ago. Besides the fact that the entire world had changed since then, there were some similarities; then, I was also alone, sans kids and husband and grateful for that. But back in February, I had been itching for an escape from family life, drowning in obligation and responsibility.

Now, though, everything was different. I actually missed Carlos and the twins, which surprised me given we had been together 24/7, surrounded by the same four walls, for the last several months. I realized, not unhappily, that I couldn't wait for them to join me in ten days' time. They'd be coming with my parents, whom I hadn't seen in eight months. While I still wasn't sure what I wanted my new real life to look like, I no longer felt such a driving and compelling need to run away from my old one.

I finished breakfast and hopped in the car at exactly 7:47. By 7:53, I was staring up at Kinloch's quintessential Scottish hunting lodge facade: white-painted front with a gabled roof, two heavy wooden double doors, and huge stag's antlers crowning the doorway. I said a silent prayer to the dead stag: *Please let me not be roadkill today.*

Isabella came straight in to greet me at the door before I had even taken off my coat. "I'm still so nervous," she said, embracing me. "Are you sure you're ready?"

"As ready as I'll ever be," I said.

She laughed and took me behind a door marked "staff only." My shift, and my new life for the next month, had begun.

For my first rotation, I was on dining duty. Kinloch's restaurant was fairly famous and had experienced many incarnations.

At its inception, it was the domain of Isabella's mother, Lady Claire, known for her homey take on Scottish cuisine. An up-and-coming Brazilian chef, Marcello Tully, took over from her; he spent more than a decade honing his immense technical skill and a grounding in fine French cuisine that earned Kinloch a Michelin star. Marcello had left earlier that year and Jordan Webb, a no-nonsense chef from Brighton who loved simple food and fresh ingredients, took over just as the first COVID wave was abating.

The warm cinnamon goodness of Kinloch's award-winning porridge wafted toward me as I passed through the swinging door. I had never been in a professional kitchen before and was struck first by how narrow the space was. The main prepa-ration and serving areas were shaped like two rectangles, a smaller one nested inside a larger exterior. The perimeter and interior were full of shelves, counters, and fridges surrounded by a very thin walkway around. Every wall, counter, and shelf space had a role and a purpose. I learned quickly that each room behind the scenes at Kinloch was like Mary Poppins's magical carpetbag: it fit more inside than one could ever imag-ine possible.

Emma, who had been with Kinloch for years and had served me in the dining room many times before, came out to say hello. Emma was local, short (the Scots would say "wee"), and usually wore her long blond hair in a braid down her back. She, along with Krissy and Jamie, whom I knew, and Kayleigh, whom I didn't yet, were the supervisors. There was always one on duty every shift to oversee every detail, and they worked across all the different areas to make sure it all ran smoothly.

"It's so weird to see youse back here," Emma said, her accent thick but clear.

"Just pretend like you've never met me before and it's my first day," I replied.

"Are you sure?" she said, an eyebrow raised.

Breakfast, she explained, was the easiest meal service of the day: choice was limited and the service was fairly standardized. Diners—almost all hotel guests—came down more or less at a scheduled time. They were offered a choice of a starter (fruit bowl, yogurt, granola, or the aforementioned heavenly porridge). Then guests would move on to the main course: a full Scottish breakfast with sausage and haggis or, if you were feeling healthy, maybe just a smoked salmon scramble.

The orders were taken by whoever was assigned the section. On that morning, there weren't many guests, so all orders were being taken by Imogen, whom I met next. She was Australian and had come over to Scotland on a two-year visa. She had long hair, dyed so red it was almost purple. Imogen was sassy, cynical, and snarky. She seemed to have a perpetual hangover and an attitude, but to her credit, both disappeared the second she went in front of a guest. She hated the COVID restrictions. "If I'm going to die," she told me, eyeing my mask, "at least I'd like to do it at a rave."

"Right," Emma told me, "you can walk through the dining room and see if anything needs to be cleared. Dishes get dropped over with Jake, but ask him where things go, he's quite particular. If you're done with that, you can polish the silverware or fold napkins."

I was taking notes, but already perplexed. Where did dirty teapots go? And who was Jake?

She nodded, as if somehow that made it easier to understand, and then hurried back to the kitchen to the call of "Service!" from the chefs, which meant that someone's food was getting cold and one of us needed to get our ass over there to serve it, pronto (my translation).

Once breakfast got started, it didn't stop for an hour and a half, but it felt like a day and a half. Everyone knew what to do: they were speeding around with purpose, while I was moving in slow motion. Anyone who has ever worked in a kitchen will tell you that it's a lot like an intricate, choreographed dance. I, unfortunately, didn't know any of the steps.

"Behind!" someone would yell, warning that they were coming up behind me, and I'd turn to look over my shoulder, nearly crashing into them. "Table 3 away for mains," someone else would yell. Did that mean the guests had left? Or their mains had left? I was so confused and worried that I was in the way. Eventually, I just hid in the corner with a mountain of silverware, polishing until I could see my reflection in it. If I couldn't manage anything else properly, at least I'd ensure people would have the cleanest forks they had ever seen.

Even with not knowing what I was doing and the beginnings of a dull ache in my feet, the experience of being behind the scenes in a working restaurant was kind of exhilarating. By the time I had dropped off the last set of breakfast dishes with Jake, I was full of adrenaline. Jake was on "KP," or dish duty. He had long strawberry-blond hair, tied up in a bun, and a matching handlebar mustache. Luckily, he didn't really seem to care very much where I put the teapots; he had the laid-back attitude of someone about to catch a wave in Sydney, not soak another round of ceramic jam spoons. "No worries," he said on repeat, every time I asked if something was okay.

I had always considered myself a whiz at multitasking, but the skill set required to be successful in a professional kitchen was very different altogether. There was so much to remember and everyone but me seemed so good at remembering. This was a place where the staff took pride in knowing the guests, and, even though everyone was masked, they could not only recite someone's room number with their eyes closed but also remember that Mrs. Jorgenson was allergic to gluten or Mr. Holmes had asked for an extra blanket. My brain was swimming with numbers and dietary restrictions and, *god*, that porridge smelled so good, when would I be able to eat some? I was starving.

Finally, the breakfast rush subsided. Emma asked if I wanted a break to eat. "Sure!" I replied, a little too loudly, walking back into the kitchen to reward myself for a hard day's work (okay, two hours'). After a meal service, any leftover food that was available to the staff was put on the "pass," a polished countertop just next to the chef's prep station—but that morning I found only a barren, silver wasteland. One slice of bacon. Half a roast mushroom. Crumbs from the buttery scones, now gone. And worst of all, no porridge. I was very glad I had eaten that egg sandwich, but I was still famished. I grabbed the bacon, scarfed it down, and got back to my tasks.

Preparations for lunch began the minute the last guest left the dining room after breakfast. Each table needed to be cleared, with new tablecloths placed and steamed. Then the tables needed to be set. Dirty tablecloths and napkins needed to be counted and bagged for the laundry. And then, Emma said, I could go home. The first half of my split shift was done.

I got into the car, massaging my aching wrists. My feet were sore and so were my ligaments. But I had done it—one whole meal service! And, most important, I had not died. I looked forward to going home and resting until my next shift started at six. It was dinner service, true, but I was convinced it would be easier now that I knew the ropes.

·········

"Here we have your home-baked raisin bread, with a beetroot-and-mackerel pâté."

"Whoops, yes, you are right, it's beetroot and goat cheese. Sorry, it's my first day."

"Can I get you anything else?"

"Something else to drink, perhaps? There's a lovely Malbec by the glass."

"Oh my, your—" said the well-mannered, impeccably dressed older English woman in front of whom I had just placed lamb three ways (roasted, confit, and in a fried ball), with a side of kale from the kitchen garden.

"My?" I looked down to see that my breast was less than a centimeter away from the long, tapered white candle on the table and starting to smoke. I didn't even know who was more embarrassed, I, who had nearly set my shirt on fire, or she, who might have had to say "boob" in public. I was completely out of my depth. Breakfast, it turned out, was like Little League. Or maybe even toddler baseball, if that's a thing. Dinner was the World Series.

Service started out quietly enough. I couldn't say I had waltzed into my six-o'clock shift cocky, but I was slightly more confident than I was that morning. I had been borderline helpful at breakfast, maybe even useful once or twice. I did not spill anything on anyone, and now, my second time around, I had the gist of the basics.

On arrival, I was greeted by Krissy, who was supervising the evening. I had known Krissy for a long time; she had been a manager at Kinloch for years. A German with piercing blue eyes and exacting standards, she looked after the restaurant and scheduling staff, managing the lodge's hiring and human resources processes. But the dining room was absolutely her domain. She was organized and meticulous and knew everything about every guest by memory. I served with all of the supervisors over the next few weeks, but no one ran a tighter ship than Krissy.

She warmly welcomed me back into the kitchen and asked how breakfast went. "Great!" I told her, enthusiastically. "But I was worried I would get a call from you over my break to say not to bother coming back in tonight; good news, I didn't."

She laughed, probably more out of politeness than anything else, and launched straight into the dinner service plan. Unlike breakfast, dinner had three courses, plus bread, after-dinner coffees and teas, petits fours, and alcoholic beverages. This meal involved the use of the till, the computer system that sent orders to the kitchen. As a backup for the technology, there was a giant whiteboard that was also used to keep track of when each table had arrived and when each course was served, so no one would be kept waiting too long. This was just called "the board," and no one ever, ever touched the board but Krissy.

I remarked that it seemed like a far more complicated affair than breakfast.

"You should have seen it before," she said. "You remember when we had Marcello's Michelin-starred seven-course tasting menus? Now it's just three starters, three mains, and three desserts. Easy. You'll be fine."

The first guests weren't due until seven, so Krissy asked me to light all the candlesticks in the dining room. The dining room at Kinloch is one of my favorite places in the entire world. The walls are a lush, dark green. Large portraits of Macdonald ancestors line each spare panel of the walls. With the soft music and the long white tapered candles bathing the

room in a soft glow, the room felt almost electric with anticipation of the meal to come. It wasn't just the food, which
looked spectacular that night—I was already salivating over
the idea of the evening's leftovers—but the ambience, the
wine, the special treatment, the whole evening was designed
as a feast for all the senses.

Guests who had the misfortune of being served by me that
evening almost definitely had not expected an experience in
which their waitress, say, set herself on fire or began to serve
their after-dinner coffee and petits fours with her fly down
(guilty) only to proceed to spill 10 percent of their cappuccino over the rim of the cup (guilty) and run out of the room,
before returning to ask the guests if she should clean it up (so
guilty, but in fairness, I didn't have a napkin *and* I had to zip
up my pants).

My first night was an unmitigated disaster. To add to my
embarrassments, there was, you know, the actual serving of
food. The chefs took great pride in how delicately they cared
for their culinary creations, and it showed. There were two
incredible mains on the menu that night: a lamb and a fish.
They were plated carefully—the cod precariously placed atop
a tall cylindrical stack of potatoes, cavolo nero, and green
beans stacked like Jenga blocks; the lamb was similarly displayed to show off its middle, so pink it looked like it had
just been slapped. They were gorgeous, but so, so fragile. One
false move and the whole thing came toppling down.

"Service!" Krissy cried from the kitchen. I looked around
to see if anyone else was going to get it. Everyone else was
occupied, busy and important, doing their jobs. I slid on my
white gloves used for serving (at this point more of a pink, as
I had accidentally dipped them in the beetroot pâté one too
many times that evening) and met her in the kitchen.

As one chef used small tongs to arrange the green bean stack just so, Krissy instructed me which way the plate should be facing when I placed it in front of the guest, for maximum appreciation of its beauty. I tried to listen, but my hands noticeably shook as I stared at the wobbling pile of delicate, exquisitely constructed food and prayed again to the stag over the front door: *Please let me not screw this up.*

The stag wasn't listening. The cod I held fell off its perch of potatoes, kale, and green beans before I had even left the kitchen, resulting in the chef making a very big show of throwing away all the food on that plate (that I would have gladly eaten myself, had it been offered) and starting again. On the second attempt, I made it a few steps farther, but the lamb, too, toppled off. I didn't have the guts to take it back to the kitchen. I set the plate down in front of the guest confidently, channeling my inner art dealer and preparing to tell them, yes, this plate of chaotic meat is supposed to look like a deconstructed Cy Twombly masterpiece.

The rest of the evening went on much in the same way. Even though I was sure no one was keeping score but me, I replayed every mistake and misstep in my head multiple times. Mostly, I just desperately wanted to be useful and not in the way. As it had been on Broadway, everyone there had a role to play and every piece of the machine had to operate correctly and collaboratively so the whole show could function. The kitchen was a bustle of activity, bright lights, and energy, the dining room calm, candlelit, peaceful. The door that swung between them was a portal between worlds. I crossed the portal, trying hard to reconcile the calm, poised person I needed to be on the outside with the frazzled klutz I felt like on the inside.

After what seemed like an eternity, the early tables were eating their dessert and there were only a few mains left to be served. Krissy told me to head home, even though the others were still busy serving.

"Is it because I'm awful?" I asked her. I knew that's what the staff were thinking. Imogen had given me a look of disgust several times already that night (legitimately, as I once forgot to catch that swinging door and it swung right into her face).

"No, not at all," said Krissy. "But you have to be here tomorrow for breakfast. And," she reminded me, "you're not getting paid for this."

She had a point. Tomorrow I got to do it all over again— because I had signed up for this! The smell of the lamb roasting in the oven floated past me as I walked to the car (or, rather, hobbled), but since dinner wasn't over yet, there were no leftovers for me. Instead I drove home, knowing there was a bowl of cold couscous waiting for me in the fridge. If, that was, I managed to get out of the car and into the house.

Chapter 15
Food, Glorious Food

The days went on and eventually things at Kinloch did get better—marginally. I became less terrible (although not, at any point, actually great), but I never stopped being completely exhausted. Hospitality was hard work, which I knew though perhaps had forgotten. While in grad school in 2003, I had been a "barmaid" at the Hogshead in London's Leicester Square. When I started there it was—and I say this affectionately—a total shithole. I did not care. It was a real English pub, just like in the movies, where a cabbie with a ruddy nose and flat cap yells over from the corner something like "Oi guvna, give us a pint" and then breaks out into song with his fellow chimney sweeps. I had zero experience at bartending and was hired only because I was young and cheerful and had a reference in the form of friends of mine who had worked there the previous summer.

My first day at the pub remains one of the most embarrassing of my life. I had just ten minutes of training, which was mostly about not drinking on the job and about using the cappuccino machine, only to be thrown behind the bar and left to my own devices. I was twenty, not even old enough to legally order a drink in America, and I had been in the UK for only a few weeks. My first customer ordered a tea with milk, so I found a tea bag and put it in a mug with some hot water. Then, assuming this was the right opportunity to show off the skills gleaned from my training, I frothed up some nice hot milky foam, like one would find in a cappuccino, and added it to his tea. Proudly, I brought it over to his table with a smile, confused when he glared back at me.

"What's this meant to be?" he asked with disgust (not an exaggeration—the English take their tea very seriously). My eyes welled with tears—"I'm so sorry, it's my first day and I'm from Miami and it's really hot there but we mostly drink Cuban coffee and I've never even drunk a cup of tea, much less made one," I wailed.

He got up from his table, this Good Samaritan, walked behind the bar with me, and showed me the proper way to make a cup of tea (tea bag steeping in the hot water first, cold milk added at the very end—although even this is controversial, as some Brits insist on cold milk first). If only that gentle gentleman had been around later that day, when I had to open my first bottle of wine and didn't realize you were supposed to take the foil cap off before pulling out the cork.

Over the next six months, I embraced that job with gusto. I can say, without being arrogant, that eventually I got really good at it. Mostly, this was because I am friendly and have always genuinely enjoyed small talk with strangers. In the early aughts, being American in a room full of Brits was an asset, not a liability. Not to mention the pub was always loud and raucous and there was a huge slip-proof mat behind the bar: If a glass falls in a noisy pub and no one hears, did it even really happen?

The job had its downsides. It was physically taxing—my (younger) feet ached back then too—and there were other unsavory elements to the job. Despite being a nonsmoker, I smelled like an ashtray 24/7, and no amount of hot water could wash off the stench. Also, a large portion of the Friday-night clientele were what we called "wanker bankers." They showed up with envelopes full of cash (from their employers, to be spent on treating their coworkers to a night out), loose morals, and very little respect for women. If I had a pound for every time I had gotten my ass pinched, I would have made a lot more each weekend than the £5.35-per-hour minimum wage.

During my tenure there, I cleaned up more vomit than anyone should have to in a lifetime. And, yes, I once had to accompany a Danish colleague—a lovely, if naïve, young woman with two long blond braids like the Swiss Miss Girl—to the emergency room after she got hit on the head with a wayward ashtray during a bar fight between rival gangs from neighboring Chinatown.

But I loved that job fiercely, mostly due to the people I worked with. So many of my fellow bartenders were travelers too, from all over the world: Israel and Ireland and Nigeria and New Zealand and South London. Some were young like me, just starting their journeys. Others had been on the road for longer. They were different from one another, but, most important, they were different from me and pretty much anyone I had known. Once the pub closed, we'd sneak glasses of whatever we knew wasn't counted during inventory—for example, anything poured out of the tap at the bar, like beer or cider, had some wastage built in, but bottled beverages got carefully tracked (though sometimes we took those anyway). Then we'd sit on the freshly wiped-down bar stools and talk about anything and everything: news, politics, books, life, whether aliens existed, or who was sleeping with Danny, the manager, that week. I probably learned more about the "real world" in those few months than I did in four years of college.

But there were some key differences between then and now. Then, I was twenty. Now, nearly forty. True, that's not at all old in the grand scheme of things, but my body did not have the same stamina it once had. Now, my hangovers took up to three days to recover from, for one thing, and my feet, less spry than they once were, were unaccustomed to eight-hour shifts. My brain, fairly skilled at multitasking, was bursting at the seams as I struggled to switch between taking lunch orders, remembering to tell housekeeping that room 12 wanted turndown service, and then, on my break, hopping on a parent-teacher Zoom call in the private dining room.

Hospitality, at least at Kinloch, felt like a young(er) person's game. My large crew of coworkers, freshly out of adolescence, did nothing to disabuse me of that notion. Because of the hotel's remote location, and the nature of hospitality jobs in general, most of the staff had come from abroad to work at the hotel for a fixed period of time. They were often from countries in the Commonwealth, places that were once British and now had special visa arrangements for young people to enable them to come to the UK and travel and work in their twenties. Australia's and New Zealand's youth mobility visas were so popular they were practically a rite of passage.

The bulk of the staff at Kinloch were no different. There were some locals, islanders or from nearby towns on the mainland, but the large majority were twentysomething Antipodeans. They moved to Skye, lived in spare rooms at the hotel or in caravans parked behind it, and worked in the restaurant or bar until it was time to move on to the next adventure. I christened them the Aussie Posse.

Imogen and Jake were both members, along with maybe a dozen others. They provided the starkest comparison to what my life once was, or certainly to what it was now. The two were half a world away from home, living in an extraordinary place with boyfriends or girlfriends and coworkers. Location-wise, they were isolated, but they had each other. And they had beer. And music. After the last table had been prepped for the following morning's breakfast, they drank and laughed and listened to bands with ridiculous names, comparing notes on the newest albums by Slut Mouth (not to be confused with Slutface), Hockey Dad, Skeggs, and Psychedelic Porn Crumpets.

My own late teens and early twenties were in some ways similar. I had plenty of fun, plenty of hangovers, plenty of ill-advised flirtations with terrible music and terrible boys. I worried about paying my rent every month, not to mention trying to keep up with the credit card debt I had accrued. I adventured too, living in London and New York, cities I had always dreamed about.

But in other ways, my twenties couldn't have been more different from the Aussie Posse's. I was on a path, a somewhat linear one that felt, even then, like it was leading somewhere. At twenty-two, I was in a steady relationship that soon turned into marriage. I had some jobs that were about paying the bills and exploring—like pint-pulling at the Hogshead—but they were part-time while I studied. Once I finished school, I dove headfirst into my career in consulting and corporate philanthropy. I finished my twenties making a good salary and with two newborns. I had no regrets, but it dawned on me that maybe my internship adventure was, in a way, about revisiting that time of my life, a time when all the pages ahead were blank and unwritten.

After eight straight days "on" at the lodge, I had completed my rotation in the restaurant and was moving over to the front of house. I'd miss the buzz of the dining room, but not the abject terror that hit me every time I heard the call "Service!" and knew I was going to have to deliver a plate of food without dropping it on someone's head.

Front of house really just meant that, instead of hanging out in the kitchen between tasks, I would be hanging out behind the bar, which doubled as the reception desk. Looking after guests' comings and goings was a big part of the job. Checkouts trickled in throughout the morning, while check-ins usually started around midafternoon. There were other small responsibilities, like ensuring the drawing rooms and the "Over By" (a second building of hotel rooms that was a few yards from the main edifice) were clear and clean, with plumped pillows and roaring fires. Another big part of the job was making and serving cocktails to guests in the front lounge, a room that would normally be packed with guests who had flocked up to Skye from elsewhere in the UK, desperate for fresh air and natural beauty. While the usual swarm of international visitors had not returned due to limitations on international travel, the Londoners were definitely here. And the Glaswegians. And the Mancunians.

It all felt refreshingly normal, but it wasn't going to last. The night before I started my front-of-house rotation, the first minister of Scotland had announced new restrictions on the hospitality industry, banning the sale of alcohol for sixteen days. No bartending for me—the one job I knew how to do— and, worse, almost no guests. Kinloch had been counting on being at full capacity in October to help it through. In the twenty-four hours after the alcohol ban was announced, there were forty-nine cancellations.

"We need to make every guest that comes feel incredibly special and that we are so glad that they have chosen to be here," Isabella told us. "And we need to pull together as a family."

She and the team had been discussing ideas to quickly adapt our service to meet the new regulations, which had a few loopholes for hotels. Alcohol could not be served inside but could be served outside. To address this, it was decided that we would launch an outdoor fire pit and a special menu of winter warmers—like hot toddies with whiskey or gin— and s'mores by the fire (my idea, although I ate more than I sold). The Aussie Posse and the others rallied with more ideas: Could we have blankets and hot water bottles? Should we assign waitstaff outside to make sure drinks were refreshed regularly? Everyone quickly closed ranks and it really did feel like a family, pulling together.

Once the meeting was over, I started walking out of the room to hang my coat. A bubbly, bouncing blonde with a local accent approached me. "Hi! I'm Kayleigh!" she said. She spoke with exclamation marks. "We'll be on front of house together today."

Kayleigh had grown up in Glenelg, a short ferry ride away from Skye on the mainland. At eighteen, she decided to see the world, working hospitality jobs in Barcelona and Bangkok and Bordeaux, only to return home when the world locked down, making her way to Kinloch and quickly rising in the ranks to become a supervisor.

Sometimes in life you meet someone and know, immediately, that the two of you are destined to be friends. That happened to Kayleigh a lot, I think. She had everything I loved in a person—energy and enthusiasm, a quick brain, a solid work ethic, and a penchant for gossip. In between notes on how to check people in and out, how to take bar orders, and how to use the birch sap tapped from the trees outside to make a killer gin cocktail, she briefed me on the current state of her affairs, and everyone else's. Besides the camaraderie and the free drinks or food (the latter of which had yet to materialize), the best part about working in hospitality was, hands down, the relationship drama. At Kinloch, a lot of this was heightened because most of the staff that came from abroad, including most of the Aussie Posse, came in pairs, with a boyfriend or girlfriend in tow.

Kayleigh had drama of her own. She had recently started a new romantic entanglement with a chef at the lodge but wasn't sure if he reciprocated her feelings. Together we analyzed every text and behavior, as she rationalized the ones she didn't like. She dropped by his room with donuts one morning that she had gone out early to retrieve—no small feat, given that getting to the closest bakery was a forty-minute round-trip journey—and he refused to open the door to her, saying he was "too tired." But, he said, she could leave the donuts outside the door. "He's got a weird relationship with his parents and that's why he acts like that," she said.

It was hard to watch a gorgeous, bright twenty-three-year-old girl get steamrolled by a classically emotionally unavailable boy. "Kayleigh," I told her, having met her only hours before but immediately destined to become her older, sage, happily married confidante, "you need to be clear about your expectations. Tell him what you want. If he doesn't want the same thing, then at least you know. But be honest with him. It's the only way."

She thought for a moment, then shook her head. "No, I think I just need to step up my game. Maybe I'll buy a new bra."

To be in one's twenties and single. What a steaming pile of heartbreak and misery; it was one thing I definitely did not miss. I polished glasses while she told me about her plans for that evening, thinking that I was so desperately glad for once that I was a little older, a little wiser, and no longer attracted to unsuitable heartbreakers.

·········

I was hoping that my big move to the front desk would make up for my crash and burn in the dining room, but it appeared that my incompetence at serving food was matched by inability to remember how to communicate with other humans. Months of working from home had left me bereft of small talk, the art of which, it appeared, I had forgotten. I welcomed two women, whom I had met a few times already over the previous shifts, as they arrived for dinner. "You've changed your kit," one said to me, referring to the face shield I was now sporting over my mask, as a nod to the rise in cases. "I like it."

"Oh, this. Yes." I sighed, tired of all the personal protective equipment I had to wear to feel safe, but generally resigned to it. "Just trying to spice things up a bit."

"Yours is nice though. No tacky letters. I had one of those face shields for work, but it just read FACE SHIELD in big letters across the top," she said.

"Maybe I should get one that says BOSS BITCH on mine."

I stood there stunned at who had said that—did the words "boss bitch" really just come out of my mouth in a professional setting?

Luckily, she roared with laughter, allowing me to hide behind the bar, keenly aware that this was not the way that nice waitstaff at nice restaurants are supposed to talk.

Another issue was checking in guests, a key part of the front-of-house job. The ideal way to do this was to be fast and unobtrusive. Guests had traveled far to get there—Kinloch was a two-hour drive from the nearest airport or major train station—and all they wanted to do was get to their rooms quickly and begin their decompression. But I couldn't seem to help it; I was very, very obtrusive. I loved the chitchat part—finding out where people were from and what brought them to Skye and telling them about my love for the place—but could not manage the other requirements, like, for example, remembering what room they checked into. In order to physically guide guests to the correct room, one had to first check the day sheet, a detailed guide to everything happening in the hotel that day, before setting off upstairs or to the Over By with their bags. Amid all the small talk, I would make it halfway down the hall before realizing I had forgotten their room number.

One memorable afternoon, the rain was falling softly outside, and I could see clouds rolling in over the loch as the Wilsons passed through the front doors. No one else was around to check them in, so it was up to me. I had shadowed a few arrivals so far, but I hadn't done one by myself yet. I felt confident though; how hard could it really be?

"Welcome to Kinloch Lodge," I said with my broadest and most welcoming smile, the one I saved for my orthodontist when I ran into him at the grocery store. "I'd be delighted to check you in today. Let me just find your room number and we'll be on our way. Do you need any help with your bags?" I asked.

Mr. Wilson eyed me up and down. He was tall, had at least fifty pounds on me, and looked strong. He, like most of the men who arrived at the lodge, seemed embarrassed to ask a woman to carry their bags. "That's fine," he said, grunting as he hoisted his bulky suitcase over his shoulder. "I'll manage."

I ran behind the bar to check the day sheet for their room assignment. I had been in the habit of forgetting people's room numbers halfway to the room, but I promised myself I would not forget this time. Wilson . . . Wilson . . . Wilson, room 4.

Four? Where was room 4? There was a cheat sheet pinned up on the board that detailed the location of each room. I knew rooms 14–23 were in the Over By, the other building that sat across the lawn; rooms 5–12 were upstairs in this building. So where was room 4?

The sheet said "out the front door around the corner." Okay, fine, I thought; I had seen some doors there but didn't know they were rooms. Must be one of those. I walked back around to see Mr. Wilson's brow sweating from the weight of his luggage.

"Right! We're all set. If you'd please follow me."

It was raining outside and we walked quickly, sans umbrellas, single file. "Four, four, four," I repeated under my breath to myself over and over. We arrived at the first door around the corner. It had no visible number. Must be room 2. That meant that room 4 was two doors down.

Certain that the number four was emblazoned on my brain, never to be forgotten for the rest of eternity, I launched into the spiel: "There is Wi-Fi throughout the property, but you don't need a password. We'd be happy to bring any drinks to your room; just dial zero on the phone for room service. There are a lot of lovely walks in the area. Ahh, here we are, room 4."

We arrived at the door that was two doors over from room 2. Confidently, I turned the knob and opened the door. Almost as quickly, I slammed it shut.

My body had blocked the Wilsons from what I had just seen: One Mr. James, a portly older gentleman, with a bristly mustache like a walrus's, had been sitting on the chaise longue, enjoying the view of the rain and the expansive lawn with a bottle of white wine. Entirely in the nude. The James party was in room 3.

"Whoops, my mistake! That's not your room. I'm so sorry. I know I don't look it, but I'm just an intern here, I don't know all the rooms yet."

I was flustered, but, overhearing me as she walked outside to toss a piece of wood in the fire pit, Kayleigh ran over to my rescue. "Hiya," she exclaimed in her cheery brogue. "Are youse the Wilsons for room 4? It's so tricky to find. It's just around the corner, follow me, I'll take you there. Here, let me grab that." Before Mr. Wilson could protest, Kayleigh had grabbed his suitcase with one arm. He audibly exhaled, both of us relieved.

Increasingly wet from our extended time in the rain, we followed Kayleigh around a second corner to room 4, where she completed the Wilsons' check-in, smoothing everything over with the promise of a complimentary cocktail. After apologizing a third time, I closed the door behind us and walked away. Kayleigh patted my back as I sank my head into my hands. "Don't worry, love," she said. "This happens to everyone."

Did it, Kayleigh? Did it really?

In spite of how truly horrible I was at a large portion of this job, I loved it. I couldn't remember the last time I had loved something I was bad at, but I truly enjoyed (almost) every minute I had been working at Kinloch. I was incompetent—but free.

For my entire life, since I was the first child in my preschool class to read (a distinction my mother still tells people about today), I have been fixated with being the best. This deep desire to always come out on top was, ironically, probably both the secret of my success and the reason for this current crisis I was mired in.

Most of the fixation was no doubt due to my upbringing. No matter whether your parents arrived by boat from Cuba or flight from Vietnam, lots of immigrant kids heard the same messages: we left everything behind so you could have a better life; education should be your single biggest priority; stop complaining about the bus, when I had to go to school it was barefoot through a field of broken glass uphill both ways.

My father's voice in my ear was part of my drive, but there was something else—something innate and deep inside of me. I got a definite dopamine bump from winning that was unlike anything else. Like any other addiction, the more I felt it, the more I wanted. I was obsessed with being number one. But looking back, this focus and desire had propelled me in one direction while cutting off other routes. Take musical theater. Sure, I was a good singer. But I wasn't the best. Part of the reason I never pursued that particular dream was because if I wasn't going to be the best at it, why do it at all?

This was probably why I was so afraid of the art world. It wasn't just Nigel and his negativity all those years ago when we met at the Tate. If curating exhibitions had been something I really wanted to pursue, I would have brushed off that meeting and found another way. But I didn't. I worried I didn't fit in.

Leaning into my strengths let me ignore my weaknesses. Yes, it allowed me to achieve and find success in the things I was good at. But I was starting to question whether I needed to be spending more time nurturing those tiny seeds of things I was terrible at—serving dinner, for example—to see if maybe they might blossom into something more, given some effort *and* some mistakes. Maybe it didn't matter if I was "the best" if I was doing something I loved. I didn't even know what being the best meant anymore in this new world.

There was something so reassuring about the world of Kinloch. Everything was so black-and-white. Guests were checking in or checking out, rooms were clean or dirty, meals were ready or not. Every single task and activity had a process behind it, and a checklist behind the process. Every item had a place. Every cupboard had a purpose. I found so much quiet joy there. During slow moments, I would dry bar glasses (breaking only one, thank you very much), fold starched napkins, or polish silverware: repetitive tasks that required just enough brainpower to accomplish what was needed so I wouldn't have to focus on the bigger questions still spiraling through my mind. Is the world collapsing? Do I take the job with Harry? What does the future hold?

One early evening, I was at the bar restocking the soft drinks when Kayleigh ran over, breathless. "Quick, come," she said and pulled me with her onto the lawn outside. Kinloch was surrounded by mountains on three sides and Loch na Dal on the fourth. The sun was about to set and the sky was burning orange, pink, and red. Everyone—the dining staff, office team, and guests—had all come outside to watch the sunset.

"Isn't it amazing?" Kayleigh asked me, at a loss for words for the first time since I met her. In spite of having spent her whole life in this part of the world, seeing sunsets like these all the time, she, and everyone else here, still took a moment to appreciate the quiet beauty surrounding them. We all stood silently outside, mesmerized, as the sun sank below the mountains. Then we went back inside to finish our shifts.

Chapter 16
Turning into the Dark

There it was, right on the day sheet, one of my favorite words in the English language: "wedding." Since I had started, the hotel had hosted two engagements (sadly, both did the actual proposing privately, depriving me of my dream of putting a ring in a chocolate mousse and anxiously hoping it wasn't choked on before the question was popped), but this was the first wedding that was actually taking place at Kinloch under my watch.

I was scheduled to work on Saturday and Sunday, my final two front-of-house sessions before I made my way into the offices on Wednesday for my final rotation. It was a full house that weekend and, in spite of the increasing restrictions, it promised to be a busy one. It was also my last few days before a life more akin to my real one returned.

I woke up late on Saturday morning and lingered for a long time over my coffee as it transitioned from hot to lukewarm to cold, watching the gray clouds move across the sky from my sofa and appreciating my last few days of quiet. My husband, children, and parents would be arriving on Monday. I hadn't seen my mom and dad since before their trip to New

York (and everything else) was unceremoniously canceled. The weekend was my last opportunity to be 100 percent focused on my work at Kinloch before diving back into my other "jobs"—mother, wife, daughter—and the responsibilities that came along with them.

Truthfully, I was looking forward to seeing everyone. I was no longer as afraid of being subsumed in these other identities and knew that the core of who I was, or whoever I was figuring out I wanted to be, at least, was strong enough to stand on its own. In fact, the heft of my obligations no longer seemed overpowering; I had started to feel comforted by them, like a weighted blanket that kept me grounded. In spite of how difficult lockdown had been, I sort of missed the mandatory family time it had forced on us. And after a year when so many were lost, I felt unbearably grateful that I still had those other identities to call my own.

My family's arrival also served as a stark and more unwelcome reminder that my internship journey was almost over. I had only a week left at Kinloch and didn't feel much closer to knowing what I was going to do afterward. I had stress dreams every night. In one, I was working on a yacht, or maybe it was a fishing boat, but the waves were so choppy I kept worrying I would fall over. Occasionally Harry or Frankie, my old internship bosses, would show up in my subconscious to assign me some work that I didn't know how to do. Sometimes, though, I dreamed I was back in my old job as CEO as if no time had passed and nothing had changed. Those were the worst of all.

Everyone at work was expecting me to come back to my old job once I finished my final Kinloch shift, and even though I didn't think that's what I wanted, I hadn't told them otherwise. I had been waiting for an epiphany, especially about

Harry's offer and whether I was really prepared to dive head-first into a new, full-time job. But no epiphany had revealed itself yet, and it wasn't going to that morning, I supposed. I looked at my phone, saw I was running late, and rushed off to work, where I was greeted by that happy word on the day sheet announcing the wedding celebration to come.

After hanging up my coat, outfitting myself with my mask and face shield that increasingly made me look like an astronaut, popping my head back into the kitchen to see what was on the dinner menu (lobster; I almost died), and getting the latest from Kayleigh (who had just discovered she had a fork in her bra and didn't know how it got there), I did a loop around the fire pit to take a few drink orders from the guests outside: the English couple (*Prosecco and a pint please, love*) who had come up from London with their three young children and were checking out the following day; a trio of boisterous American men (*Gin and tonics and keep 'em coming*), who couldn't remember how they became friends—or at least wouldn't tell—who were sticking around; and, of course, the wedding party, who had all arrived together.

The grooms, Ian and John, had descended with their tiny entourage of four. Weddings were restricted to fifteen guests at that point, but I got the feeling that even if they had been able to invite more, they might not have. Both men were young, probably in their early to mid-twenties, with curly hair (Ian's blond, John's brown), and flanked by a fierce quad of protective friends, including Louise, who was clearly in charge of the nuptial planning. While checking them in, I noted three things: 1) There were no parents. This wedding appeared to be happening without the support of their families. 2) They were extremely price-sensitive and this weekend would be a splurge for them. And 3) no pandemic or crumbling world around them could detract from the fact that the grooms were clearly, madly in love and could not believe their luck to have found each other and to be sharing their special day in the natural splendor that Kinloch offered.

Kayleigh had asked me to be the point person for their party for the weekend, so I introduced myself and said that I would be there for anything they needed. If I was going to do one thing right during this internship, I privately decided, it was going to be making this wedding the most incredible experience of their lives.

I love weddings about as much as the average red-blooded American woman, which is to say, a lot. Not only did I dream of my own as a little girl, doing the requisite pillowcase on the head (which made me look more like a nun than a bride, but since I was marrying the dog, it didn't really matter), but I also spent many formative hours consuming a borderline unhealthy amount of wedding-related content: reality shows like *Say Yes to the Dress* and *Perfect Proposal* and movies like *Father of the Bride* and *Four Weddings and a Funeral* (which I had to watch with subtitles until I moved to the UK and could finally understand a sober Glaswegian—barely). I was enamored with the idea of soul mates and true love and blah blah blah, but it was the party that I was the most into, alongside the idea that it was *your* day (or in my case, *mine*). You could make everything you wanted a reality, including custom M&M's with your face on them, and no one could tell you otherwise. In my dreams, my future groom and his (incorrect) opinions never factored into the equation.

My own wedding, while not actually perfect, lives in my memory as untouchable as the Hope Diamond. Yes, there were fights with my parents about budget and whom to invite (or cut), a minor freak-out over my hair on the morning of (assuaged with a well-timed bottle of champagne), and a hilarious conversation between my wedding planner and my father-in-law, where she asked him if he needed socks and he heard something *very* different; but those things are wisps of memory. What I remember the most (besides looking smoking hot) was feeling so lucky to have all the people I loved in one place (celebrating me, natch), something that I supposed wouldn't happen again until my funeral, and then I wouldn't get to enjoy it.

It made me even more determined that Ian and John would have the best day of their lives. Anyone who has ever been to a British wedding, large or small, knows there is just one secret to that: lots and lots of alcohol.

The morning of their wedding day was gray and overcast, but the weather reports said the rain wasn't supposed to start until four. With their ceremony scheduled for two o'clock, that gave them enough time for a few hours of outdoor drinking before they had to come inside and follow the restrictions on alcohol consumption. At around one, they came down to the lobby in their finery, the whole wedding party dressed to the nines. The grooms wore matching beige suits; Louise was in a floor-length beaded lilac dress. I saw them coming and popped the first bottle of champagne so it was ready for their arrival.

"You're such a doll!" Ian exclaimed. "Please come drink with us later."

"Is this included in what we paid for?" Louise whispered anxiously.

"Not to worry," I told her. "It's on the house."

I poured their glasses and then came back with the cork. "I thought you might want this," I told John, handing it to him. "To remember the day." He looked like he was going to cry.

The celebrant who was there to officiate the wedding arrived and the event began. The other guests at the hotel, also sitting outside enjoying the mild day and ability to have an al fresco cocktail, stood up to watch as Louise walked Ian down the lawn, Pachelbel's Canon in D playing in the background, to where an emotional John was waiting. Without warning, I burst into tears. My face shield fogged up and I had to go inside and compose myself.

While the ceremony was taking place, I rushed to their rooms to clean out all the glasses and bottles left there. There were at least fifty. It took me four trips back and forth from the Over By to the bar to clear them all. I think they had embraced the adage "Start as you mean to go on."

Once the grooms had kissed and been pronounced Mr. and Mr., there was a lot of tearful hugging. Hugging—remember hugging?—seemed like a relic of a bygone era. Mist was rolling in over the loch and we knew the weather wouldn't hold out much longer, but there was still time for more champagne. I brought out the second bottle. Then the third. On my way back and forth between the lawn and the bar, the three American men stopped me. "Send them a bottle of what they are having from us," one of them told me. On my way out with that bottle (four), the English couple, having their pint and prosecco outside with their son, asked me to do the same. That was number five.

By this point things were getting sloppy, but in a beautiful, emotional way. Louise had to sit down, as Kayleigh brought her some hot coffee and a plate of roast potatoes from the staff dinner (leftover Sunday roast, incredible) to sober her up. I brought Ian and John the bottles.

"These are from those two groups of guests," I said, pointing them out and beaming with a renewed sense of faith in humanity.

Ian's eyes filled with tears. He hugged me. I hadn't gotten a hug from a stranger in eight months. "I'm just so happy," he said. "This is the greatest day of my life."

Mission accomplished. Finally, after two long weeks of screwing things up, I had done something really, really right.

·········

After the wedding I took Monday and Tuesday off to welcome the rabble home. My whole family arrived without a hitch, in spite of all the new barriers that had been erected to prevent international travel. After testing, isolating, and worrying, everyone was together. My mom gave me a huge hug as she arrived. "You look different," she remarked. "Relaxed." The house quickly filled with noise, but I didn't miss the quiet—it was joyful to have everyone in one place again.

On Wednesday I was back at it, in the Kinloch office for my final rotation. In just over a week, my internship would be complete. Actually, all of my internships would be complete. I didn't have anything else lined up and had not yet responded to Harry's job offer. I needed to make a decision soon, but wasn't sure what that decision was going to be.

The office at Kinloch was the place where everything ended up. Isabella told me even before I started that it embarrassed her; it was unfinished. They had always meant to refurbish it, but the areas that guests would see wound up taking precedence. It was total chaos, yes, but organized chaos. My favorite kind.

I was back in my comfort zone—in front of a computer in an ergonomic chair—and glad to be able to bring my organizational prowess to bear. And to spend a lot of the day sitting. My first task was filing, big stacks of booking requests and, with a heavy heart, an equally large stack of cancellations. There were just two scant binders that contained every cancellation that had been processed from 2016 to 2019. For 2020 alone, eight binders had already been filled to bursting, one per month since March. The notes were emotional. Coming to such an extraordinary but remote place like Kinloch was a dream trip for many. One read, "I'm a young father and have been saving for eighteen months to bring my family to Scotland. Now my job is at risk and I'm not sure when we'll be able to come." They were only printed-out emails, but the disappointment, worry, and regret seeped through the typeface. I was, not for the first time, reminded of how incredibly lucky I was to be there.

I spent two days reorganizing all the files and was inordinately proud of myself. Proud of my accomplishments, I took a photo of my handiwork and sent it to my dad.

"I have never doubted your ability to file," he deadpanned.

Isabella was in and out most days but always made a point to catch up with me when she came in. Close to my final day, she brought her two sons over to meet me. They were tall, handsome teenagers, with boy-band haircuts, both extremely polite. After they left, she pulled me aside. "Luke, my youngest, was dying to meet you," she said. "He's completely fascinated by you. 'Have you seen her résumé?' he keeps asking me. 'Why is she clearing plates and filing?' He doesn't get it! He thinks you are so impressive, but he can't figure out why you would want to come work here."

It was a throwaway conversation for Isabella, quickly forgotten, but Luke's words fell on me like the cod off a perfectly prepared pile of vegetables. When I finished my shift that day, I got into the car and sat with the key in the ignition, not turning it, for a good long while. Luke's question was the same one everyone had been asking me since my internship journey began: Why are you doing this? Why would you even want to? It was impossible for people to fathom why I would want to leave what I already had—my CEO role, control of my own days—for unpaid internships.

My own questioning, though, over the last few months, was different from Luke's. It wasn't "Why was I doing this?" but "Why was it that, in spite of the fact that I was doing tasks I put behind me years ago (filing, dusting, writing emoji-filled social media posts, picking up trash, finishing each day with my body bruised and feet aching), I had been having the best time of my life? Why had I felt freer and younger than I had in years?"

This year, 2020, was a year that for most people will go down among the worst of their lives, and for good reason. I never once forgot the uniqueness and privilege of my position to take this journey—at any time, really, but particularly in a year like this one. But, in spite of a year full of darkness, I had been given the most extraordinary gift, and it had come in the guise of these unpaid, emotionally taxing, physically exhausting, internships.

I loved every single one of them, not because they all turned out to be my dream job—most of them didn't—but because they were different and new. They forced me to be uncomfortable, to *not* be the expert in the room. They challenged me to develop skills that were rusty and learn new things, from researching the provenance of million-dollar paintings to carrying dirty lunch plates. I had to pay close attention. I couldn't phone it in. I had to take small tasks that in my "real life" I had come to find tedious and do them with care. And to truly, genuinely find joy in completing them.

A few years back, I had a client, a young woman who had inherited a substantial amount of money. She was quirky and into alternative therapies, having spent a formative few weeks at an ayahuasca retreat in Peru. The leader of that retreat was passing through London, and my client, whom I had been advising on philanthropy for a few years by then, asked me to join them for the day. Once I ascertained that there was no requirement to actually drink ayahuasca in her living room, I said yes. I couldn't really have said no. Consulting is not unlike hospitality in that way: the customer is always right.

This shaman was a middle-aged guy from somewhere in the north of England and had set for us a number of nonhallucinogenic activities aimed at figuring out the answer to a deceptively simple question: What is your calling? I was generally not a fan of the touchy-feely stuff (*No thanks, I do not feel like I need to pretend to have a fake conversation between myself as a child and my mother as a child*), but I was able to articulate my calling very quickly: To find joy in everything I do. And to help others find it, too.

"Joy"—such a simple, small word that holds so much complexity. It's more than happiness. It's ebullience. It's celebration. A party all day, every day, where everyone is invited. People think joy is elusive, and they're right; its impermanence is what makes it all the more important to cultivate, nurture, and appreciate it whenever it comes your way. I had always prided myself on joy being my guiding star, the fundamental tenet on which I had built not just my career but my life.

Back when I was making the early, joy-driven choices in my relatively carefree career, I didn't realize that life was short and unpredictable. Who in their twenties does? But as I aged, I came to know that nothing is guaranteed. If you wanted to enjoy as much of life as possible, you had to put some intentionality behind seeking joy. You had to pay attention. If you didn't it was likely to slip through your fingers.

Back at Kinloch, as I got ready to move the car, it really hit me. It wasn't going to be enough to take a vacation from my real life. I needed to make some changes. Big ones. I had to seek out that joy again, even if it wasn't going to be simple or easy or straightforward to do so. I reached for the gear, put the car in reverse, and then promptly put it back in park. I had left my phone inside.

I walked back in as the sun was setting to retrieve it from the staff room. In the window of the drawing room, bathed in a golden glow of light, were Ian and John. The lingering notes of "Dream a Little Dream of Me," sung by Ella Fitzgerald, could be heard in the quiet night air. The grooms rested their heads on each other's shoulders and closed their eyes.

Getting married during a pandemic required the most unbelievable optimism—and, to do it against the wishes of your family, great courage too. Despite all of the discouraging signs the universe had been sending our way, they chose to make a commitment, to double down on a future in which they would be together. They chose to be happy. To seek their joy, even if the path ahead was murky and unclear.

Phone in hand, I stole one more glance over my shoulder at their mutual reverie, before turning the key in the ignition and driving home.

·········

On my last day as a Kinloch intern, Kayleigh stuck her head around the corner to see if I needed any help. I was in a dress, a poor sartorial choice, given I had been sent that day to organize an eight-by-eight closet full of hundreds of binders. I was, as always, sweating under my mask. I know it doesn't seem like filing should be a physical activity, but the way I was doing it could have qualified me for the Olympics (or at least regionals).

I had been in that room for hours, which was probably why Kayleigh had been dispatched to make sure I was alive. In spite of the weather getting increasingly frigid outside—it was late October but felt like winter—it was boiling in the closet. Some of the files hadn't been touched since they were originally deposited in there a decade or more earlier.

"I'm fine!" I called from my perch.

Kayleigh raised an eyebrow.

My right foot was up on the second shelf and my left was another two shelves higher as I stretched my fingers to grab a set of tax records from 2011. I did not look fine. But even with paper cuts and dust in my nail beds and a glistening brow, I was. More than fine.

Isabella's son's words, and my subsequent realization, had been ringing in my ears almost nonstop. I heard them as I brushed my teeth in the morning and took my vitamins before bed. They popped into my head unwanted and unbidden at four in the morning, when I struggled to sleep. "Great, so you need a change," they said. "What happens now?"

I still had no plans. I hadn't given Harry an answer or my own team any indication I wasn't coming back. The world around me was entirely uncertain, but I couldn't use that as an excuse any longer. There were decisions I was capable of making but afraid to.

Isabella had a surprise in store for me, delivered on my last day: a weekend as a guest. My not-so-subtle pleas of desperation to enjoy the food that we were serving ("Who do I have to murder to get a bit of that pork belly?" I exclaimed, out loud, more than once) had not gone unnoticed. She knew my wedding anniversary was the following week and that my parents were in town, giving me a rare opportunity for free babysitting. Did I want to come with Carlos for a weekend away? She hadn't finished the sentence before I screeched, "Yes, yes, a thousand times yes." A night alone with my husband sounded heavenly, plus I hoped that some unstructured time for quiet repose would shine a light on some of the answers I had been seeking.

On Saturday afternoon it was pouring rain but we could not have cared less. We were childless and fancy-free. We pulled into what I had now come to think of as "my" parking lot and walked into the front room. Emma was there to welcome us, as she had dozens of times before, but this time, I knew the drill.

"Do you want me to check myself in?" I asked.

"Sure, if you want," she offered, happy to indulge me showing off my new skills.

We made our way to our room. It was 19, my favorite room, the best in the house, and one I thankfully knew how to get to. The centerpiece was a claw-foot bathtub set on a platform so it matched the exact height of the rooftop window. Sitting in that bath, one had an unspoiled view of the loch and the mountains, any stray deer that found their way onto the lawn, and the wild weather on the horizon. I immediately filled the tub with bubbles and dove in for a soak. Nothing had ever felt more luxurious.

Being a guest again after weeks on staff was different but mostly the same. True, the people serving me were now my friends, but otherwise it felt comfortingly familiar. My husband and I had sat at those tables countless times before, plotting dreams and future plans. It was in that very dining room where, a year back, we discussed the internships, when they still seemed like wild fantasy. It was fitting to be back there just as my final internship was coming to a close.

I ran my finger around the rim of the wineglass, appreciating its fragility (when I broke one the previous week, I had to list it, embarrassingly, on the "wastage sheet," with my name next to it, for all to see). Someone had just filled it up without me noticing. My husband and I were the last two people left in the dining room and, it felt like, the world.

"Wouldn't the easiest thing be to just slot right back into my normal life?" I asked him.

"Probably," he said. "Is that what you want?"

"No!" I exclaimed. My mouth had beaten my brain to the punch, but it was true. It was the last thing I wanted.

"So," he said, "what's stopping you this time?"

He had asked me that question more than a year before, as we sat on our deck and tears salted up my cappuccino. And here he was, asking it again. And the answer was the same. "Nothing."

There it was. Not perhaps a grand epiphany, like uncovering the theory of relativity or inventing the lightbulb, but, in a way, it was the one I had been seeking. Nothing was stopping me from changing my life but me. So, at that moment, I decided I was going to change it. In a big way.

My entire life I had been moving in the direction I assumed was the right one, and at the time, it was. I had gotten to the place I was supposed to be, the place everyone thought I should be, and while I didn't regret a single stop on the journey, I didn't want to be there anymore. So where did I want to be?

Honestly, if truth be told, I wanted to continue being an intern.

Well, not exactly. I was done with the more exhausting elements of it, but the spirit of it was something I wanted to hold on to. To embody. I didn't want to have to keep taking side paths and then retracing my steps back to the main road. I wanted the detours to *be* the main road. Over the past few months, I had finally gotten, for brief moments in time, the chance to be the versions of myself I had seen in the shadows of my memories. I loved the chance to step into their shoes, but I didn't want to be any of them, really. I wanted to be original me, but with the freedom to take the pieces from each and carry them with me as I continued on ahead.

Each of my internships had sparked something in me I thought I had buried. My brief stint backstage in the theater reawakened in me the passion I once had for right-brained, creative activities, a passion I thought I had lost. And watching John and James direct their productions, bringing things together in a way that only legends in a field can, showed how much I craved having people to learn from. Working with Frankie at Retroglow did not just carry me through an emotionally impossible time, but as I watched her embrace the pivot, I remembered the excitement of being part of something that's still unwritten. Contemporary art gave me the confidence that I could actually apply my skills and experience to another completely different field, and maybe even make a career out of it. And my precious time at Kinloch, the stolen moment between what would eventually be two grueling lockdowns—it reminded me that it was okay to fail and be terrible at something (or everything). It was probably a good idea to put myself in positions where I could fail every once in a while.

I appreciated the opportunity to keep striving and trying new things, seeking joy wherever I could find it. I was painfully aware that to even have the option, practically and financially, to step off the treadmill made me part of a very privileged few. But if I could embody the intern spirit for a little while longer, well, why shouldn't I?

I didn't want a new job. I didn't know what I really wanted to do next. For the first time, I didn't have a plan, a charted career path. To paraphrase Cinderella in my new friend James Lapine's show *Into the Woods*, I knew what my decision was: it was not to decide. And, I realized, that that was going to be okay.

I didn't really know what any of this was going to mean in practical terms. But, in emotional ones, it felt really right.

When we woke up at Kinloch on Sunday morning, it was still raining, but everything felt clean and new. The storm had cleared a lot of the debris, both outside of the lodge and inside my head; ahead there was a glistening path, even if it was covered in fog. Plus finally, *finally*, I was going to get to sit down and enjoy a full Kinloch meal again.

I gorged myself on Sunday lunch, so full that I couldn't eat again until the next afternoon. The team kept bringing out extras: Scotch eggs from dinner the night before, seconds of the potato-and-leek soup, extra cauliflower cheese. It was gluttonous and glorious. By the time we finished dessert and tea and petits fours and extra petits fours, and they almost had to bring out the forklift to get me to the car, it was dark outside. It was nearly November, and the sun was setting by four o'clock; at four thirty it was well and truly dark.

There is a long, single-track road between Kinloch and the main road. We said our goodbyes to everyone and I pulled out of the hotel's parking lot, emerging into darkness. The Skye sky at night is a uniquely deep kind of dark that sucks in light like a black hole. On a rainy night, you may be able to see only five feet in front of you.

Trees hung over both sides as we made our way down the road, me driving like an old granny, squinting and leaning forward, nearly pressing my nose to the windshield to make sure a rogue deer didn't jump into my path.

I rounded a bend and crossed the small bridge, just wide enough for exactly one car, that covers a tributary. The water, which collects from the mountains and empties with force into Loch na Dal, was torrential that night because of all the rainfall. After I crossed the bridge, the car climbed the steep hill, followed by a sharp turn, and came up to the intersection with the main road.

Even though I had done that drive dozens of times in the past several weeks, I always found turning onto that road at night both terrifying and exhilarating. Unless there is a car coming in either direction, its headlights providing some illumination, the blackness is deep and absolute. On a cloudy night, when the moon and stars are obscured, I could barely make out my hands on the steering wheel; the glow from the dashboard was the only source of light.

On this night, like every night I had left Kinloch in the dark, I hesitated as I put my foot on the gas pedal to accelerate into the darkness. There wasn't anything to rationally be afraid of—I knew intellectually that the road was there and that it was empty—but it was so very dark. Making that blind turn was like launching into an abyss.

But tonight, the hesitation lasted a mere moment. Decision made, I pressed the gas pedal. While my path ahead was still dark, at least I was on the road now, headed in the right direction.

Afterword
Us, Ten Years Ago

Explaining to people that I was going to "embody the spirit of the intern" was not easy to do. It didn't roll off the tongue, for one thing, and moreover it didn't mean much to anyone besides me. It was the last possible thing old Alisha would have done: not make a plan, not make a list, go with my gut, and just put one foot in front of the other, even if I wasn't sure I was ready for it, to keep myself moving in the right direction. Each decision, big or small, was the equivalent of buying a nonrefundable plane ticket (something that post-pandemic I would likely never do again). I took small step after small step until eventually I looked back at the path, and I had traveled a long way indeed.

The first big decision: I took the job with Harry, with a few caveats. I wanted to do it part-time and on a six-month contract, so we could make sure it was what we both wanted. As a director of his new art-dealing business, my job was mostly to manage special projects—planning a post-lockdown exhibition in Switzerland, building out a new website, learning about anti-money-laundering regulations for the art market,

or creating an investment presentation. Part of my responsibilities also included doing regular research and ordering
books whenever a new, important piece of work came into
our orbit for sale. This involved occasional conversations
with Elodie, the lovely woman from Thomas Heneage, and we
became friendly, signing our emails with "Warmly," instead
of the cold, impersonal "Best." I even learned to abbreviate
"catalogue raisonné" as CR and drop it into casual conversations, even though privately I never stopped thinking about
Raisinets.

I wasn't sure if contemporary art was a career I wanted to
seriously pursue, but working with Harry was a comfortable
place to land from my giant leap. It was fun, challenging, and
intellectually stimulating without being overwhelming. Most
of all, it was brand-new. I was learning something every single
day. And I got paid to do it.

Besides working for Harry, my other internships, too,
kept pulling me back in. Frankie called regularly for advice
on Retroglow. The company was growing and thriving. While
planning a post-lockdown return to in-person classes, the
virtual classes were still hugely popular. Frankie had hired
additional perky instructors to help teach so she could spend
more time running the business. It was wonderful to be part
of one pandemic success story.

At Kinloch, things were still challenging with another long
lockdown in the cards, but the Macdonald clan had weathered
worse during their hundreds of years of history (including the
original plague). Isabella's resilience was an inspiration. She
spent lockdown planting tomatoes and rhubarb, foraging for
scurvy grass and mushrooms, and drying seaweed. While she
never invited me back to work a dinner shift again, she did ask
me to write and develop their new communications materials

and provide ad hoc marketing and PR support. I intentionally schedule every in-person meeting around lunchtime—they added a langoustine mac and cheese to the menu that I'd sell my firstborn for.

And as for the theater? Well, it took much longer for Broadway and off-Broadway theaters to reopen than I think anyone could have anticipated. I can only assume that's the only reason they haven't yet called, asking for their best water jug filler back. But without question, musicals needed to remain a big part of my personal and professional life. Both *Flying Over Sunset* and *Assassins* finally opened in the fall of 2021. Reviews of *Flying Over Sunset* were mixed, and a lack of raves plus a new COVID surge meant the show closed early. *Assassins* was a huge hit and even managed to extend its run by an extra few weeks due to demand. Both teams are onward and upward now to the next thing. That's show business for you.

Spending time exploring my newfound pursuits involved making space, in my life and in my head, once again. So the second big decision I made was to step down from my CEO role and transition out, passing the job on to my next-in-command. She was perfect for the job, but it's never easy to cleave yourself from a company you founded. I would still be involved, but at board level only. I was worried this decision would spark fear and panic among my team and was disappointed only for a fraction of a second when it didn't. The new generation was ready to take the reins, and I, finally, felt ready to hand them over.

One of the things I appreciated most about being an intern was the ability to *not* feel overwhelmed by my mental load. Making space meant that, all of a sudden, my brain had more room to think about other things and to consider other possibilities. Ideas for new projects sprang up like daffodils in the springtime. There was a lot in there that had been obscured by the constant to-do lists. My internships had given me a chance to see those things clearly. I didn't know what it would be like—or even what I would be like—not feeling constantly filled to capacity or, worse, overflowing at every given moment, but I was excited to find out.

The third big decision was more monumental. After thirteen years, we decided to leave London and move to Scotland. The plan was to ride out the continued pandemic at our house on the Isle of Skye, where Kinloch, Kayleigh's love life, and, most important, the mac and cheese were all only a six-minute drive away. Once things settled down and we came up for air, we'd see where the road took us. Probably a city, like Edinburgh. Maybe somewhere else. But we were going to stay put in our rural retreat for a while longer. Determined to blend in with the locals, I joined a group of women, an Extreme Friday Club, that planned weekly outdoor adventures. We scrambled over rocks through the snow to swim in a cave and kayaked to a coral island. My comfort zone was so far in the distance, I needed a telescope to see it. For his part, Carlos was even planning on doing an internship of his own, with the local coffee roasters. I was starting a movement.

No one makes the decision to move lightly, especially when you have kids and, even more so, in the middle of a pandemic, and we were no exception, lest you believe that it was a spur-of-the-moment choice, like changing from heels to flats at the last minute (always a good idea, don't ever not do this). But it took finishing my internships and realizing that I was ready for a major change for us to finally make it official.

Few things enable you to reflect back on your journey quite like moving. Moving is like telling the story of your life through the medium of stuff. Mostly crap. How did you manage to amass so much of it? Hidden among the piles of old bobby pins, unused antiwrinkle creams, and more children's artwork than would fill the Guggenheim (if the Guggenheim was filled with terrible art—sorry, kids), there were plenty of memories. The great books you read and the ones you didn't remember and thought you should probably read again (but never will). The quiet victories (like the medal I found in my nightstand drawer, commemorating the one and only time I have or will ever run a 5k), the abandoned hobbies (under my bed, I found a half-knitted baby blanket to celebrate the birth of my friend's daughter, who just turned six), and, of course, the items that elicited both happiness and heartbreak too.

In spite of truly feeling ready for what our new life in Scotland would bring, I demurred when our London landlord called to ask if I could meet the new tenants, who wanted to come by and take some measurements. My husband offered to greet them instead, ostensibly to see if they wanted to buy our curtains or any of our furniture, but really because he was nosy and curious about what they were like. He called me after they left. "They weren't what I expected," he said. "A brother and a sister and their partners. They were probably in their early to mid-twenties."

They were very polite, he said, and complimentary, which pleased my husband, who took after his mother in pride for his home and love for an obscenely unnecessary number of pillows. "Yeah, really different from us. I think it would have been harder if they had been more similar to us when we moved in. Maybe with a young kid or starting a family. You know, like us, ten years ago."

Us, ten years ago. I hadn't thought about myself ten years ago in a long time, but it came flooding back: Our own migration to that house. Me, seven months pregnant and nervous about everything, after the sadness of previous loss and the tough road to becoming a mother. When it came to moving day, my husband wouldn't let me lift a finger—I was already high-risk, plus grouchy—so I sat on the floor of the new home, laptop resting on my belly, binge-watching a pirated version of *The O.C.* that had Swedish subtitles (I learned several Swedish synonyms for "skank" that year). There I remained for most of the day, as boxes piled up one by one.

Along with the pots and pans we received as wedding gifts, and the sofa we got on sale because it was the showroom model, we brought all our hopes and dreams. I was twenty-nine, ready to start a family and a new chapter of our lives.

Flash-forward a whole decade. When we moved in, we had so much empty space that I could never imagine that house being full. Now I was spending a large chunk of my days trying to get stuff out of the house. Those pots and pans from our wedding were long gone, but the sofa, ravaged by two children who often mistook it for a trampoline, and a puppy who more than once thought it was a toilet, was still around. Ten years ago, I was working at the bank but wondering what my next challenge, after motherhood, would be. Now I had climbed up the ladder and was preparing to climb down again or, maybe, just leave the ladder altogether.

So much around me had changed, but I had changed, too. I caught a glimpse of myself in the living room mirror as we took it down from the wall to pack up. I did look different than I had ten years ago. A few more lines on my face. My hair graying around the temples. I was older. But I was still so young. And I still had a lot to do.

On reflection, I had been changing for a long time, gravitating toward a less intense, more thoughtful way of life without even realizing it. Some of the changes I made had been proactive, like becoming an intern. But thanks to the pandemic, many were reactive. I was forced to make the best decisions with the facts that I had in the situation given. The reactive changes were tough, but, in general, the proactive ones were much, much harder to make.

Changing your life *is* hard. I can see why more people don't bother. In my case, the year had taught me that there were plenty of things that didn't have to be part of my story anymore. Being a control freak—once a source of pride—was ultimately unsustainable. Overscheduling myself to the point of exhaustion didn't make me more productive or efficient as much as it had made me a terrible friend. Maybe I didn't need to be defined by my achievements and how fast I could get there, but instead by what brought me joy and happiness and inspired my passions. I had always considered myself a practical, type-A, left-brained person who needed a plan and a schedule to succeed. I still loved a plan and a schedule, but I tried, with time, practice, and a pinch of salt, to need them less.

I would never be punctual though. Some things are too deeply embedded to change.

Each of my internships taught me so much, and not just about how to use emojis or carry three plates in one hand or price a painting or fill a water jug. They taught me about their worlds. They gave me permission to adopt a different version of myself for a short time. And they taught me so much about myself: what I was capable of, what was and wasn't a core part of who I was. I learned that where I'd set my limits was sometimes arbitrary and that, ultimately, it really was me who was creating those limits. I didn't know much about what the next chapter of my life would hold, but I knew I needed to embody the spirit of being an intern in whatever I did: be adaptable; learn to fail; be okay with not being the best; let go of the plan sometimes; and above all, listen, learn, and find joy in every day.

Closing the London chapter of my life, the last ten-plus years, was emotionally difficult and sad, in spite of how ready I was to move on to the next one. There were a lot of tears, guilt over uprooting the kids from their school, sadness at leaving friends, and coworkers I would miss. But instead of putting it away in one of my patented little boxes, I let myself feel it—really feel it. There were lots of moments when it just seemed like it would be easier if I let my old life pull me back instead. My new life was like a new pair of jeans that didn't quite fit yet. They were tight, clingy, chafing in all the wrong places (but one wonders, are there right places to chafe?). But I knew deep down that they would loosen. And, soon, they'd feel comfortable too.

This analogy works the other way too: When jeans get too comfortable, they get loose and baggy. They don't fit anymore, they no longer make your tush look really cute, and you spend your whole day pulling them up. When they get too comfortable—that's when it's time to get a new pair.

On my last day in London, I did one final sweep of the old house to make sure I had taken care of everything on my list. As I peeked into each empty room to turn off lights and look in closets one last time, I could see all of the different versions of myself around me. They were all coming with me, of course. They were part of my story. But I wasn't thinking about them anymore, or the versions of me I had glimpsed on the road behind me. This change was about imagining the version of myself on the road ahead, the version I had yet to meet, and giving her the freedom to decide who she wanted to be—intern or CEO—without the expectations of the past holding her down.

Acknowledgments

Oh my god, this is so unexpected. I'm truly surprised, I didn't even prepare a speech, but I think the first thing I have to say is I can't believe I just won a Tony. I mean, wrote a book.

The first people I need to thank are the coffee growers and baristas everywhere around the world who have contributed both to my caffeine addiction and to the production of this book.

People say it takes a village to write a book, but I would actually say that *My What If Year* took a small metropolis, and I'm grateful to every single person who helped me turn this insane idea into a reality.

This book would not be a book without Stephany Evans at Ayesha Pande Literary, who read the Raisinet anecdote and responded to my cold query. Thank you for believing in me and this story and for all the happy faces you dotted along my draft.

#TeamZibbyBooks, where to even begin? I have a sneaking suspicion that publishing a book is actually nothing like this anywhere else and you've all spoiled me forever. Maybe that is the point? All of you are incredible and I feel so lucky to be a part of your squad. Leigh Newman, your patience and no-BS counsel have made this book what it is. Thank you for pushing me to mine the depths, question myself, and not rely on the easy jokes. You have made me a better writer. And Zibby Owens—Zibby!!—thank you for taking an interest in my work, believing in me, championing this book and all the writers you come across: you are a gift.

My fellow ZB authors: your memes, texts, Zoom mimosas, and words of encouragement made this process a joy. I can't wait to devour all of your books. Spring '23 WhatsApp group—Jane Delury, Andrea Dunlop, Meg Tady, Sandra Miller and Mary Otis—thanks for talking me off a ledge more than once; and Julie Chavez, my podcasting partner in crime, thank you for every check-in and Canva tutorial and my new favorite sweater.

It was never obvious to me that I would be able to actually write a book, and there were many teachers and fellow writers who spurred me along with wisdom and advice. "The Memoirists" at Faber Academy, especially Rachel Holmes; and Donna Kaz and our workshop cohort—thank you all for the free therapy. To other authors and "book people" who got on the phone when I was feeling lost, taught me excellent things about writing and even said some nice things about me to boot—Elissa Bassist, Marisa Lee Bolssen, Bianca Bosker, Becky Cooper, Mitchell Kaplan, Alicia Menendez, Eve Rodsky—thank you, thank you, thank you.

People have asked me how I got the internships and I answer: pure nepotism. A ridiculous number of people took a chance on me and gave me a peek behind the curtain: John Weidman, John Doyle, James Lapine, Darren Katz, and the casts and crews of *Assassins* and *Flying Over Sunset*. Frankie Taylor and everyone who set foot inside the virtual retro fitness time tunnel. Harry Blain, Masha, Becky, and, yes, even you,

Rebel. Isabella Macdonald and the entire extended Macdonald/ Kinloch family, including but certainly not limited to Jordan, Jamie, Krissy, Emma, Rachel, and all the guests who had the misfortune of crossing my path. I will be grateful to you all for the rest of my days and am happy to return the favor if any of you fancy an internship at whatever job it is I do now.

To the women in my life who came into this story at different times with cocktails, edits, suggestions, title considerations, dinners, and friendship. Rebecca Stone and Laura Weidman Powers, I blame everything that happened after the Coral Room on you. Nathalie Jordi, Vanessa Nadal, Joni O'Sullivan—thanks for your eagle eyes on everything. My lifelong friends, you are my sisters from other mothers, and I love you dearly.

I had the impeccable timing to write this book in the middle of a pandemic. Heartfelt thanks to the NHS and the essential workers who kept us healthy and running during that awful time and always.

To those that held down the fort while I was away, particularly Roberta Chiroli—a gifted filmmaker and photographer who just happened to be my nanny and watched my kids while I was off on my adventures—and Emily Collins-Ellis, Rachel Stephenson Sheff, Lauren Gross, and the entire I.G. Advisors team. Thank you for everything.

To the Abrams, Fernandez, and Miranda clans, thank you for your love and support. To my brothers Ted (and Lee!) and Joey, thanks for a childhood and adulthood full of hilarious anecdotes to include in here. Love you.

T&L—you're the reason for it all and being your mom is the greatest accomplishment of my life, even more than finally mastering carrying three plates at once. I can't wait for your own respective memoirs one day (or can I?).

Mommy (copy editor extraordinaire) and Papi, all of this is down to you. You have championed and supported me, humored my various indulgences, and helped me believe in myself and my work every day of my life. I'm sorry I still don't know how to use a comma appropriately, but in all other respects, I think you have succeeded. Words are not enough to express my gratitude to you, for everything.

And finally to Carlos, my partner on this adventure whether he likes it or not. There is no limit to my love and gratitude for you. Can't wait for all the What If years to come.